THE MIND OF BUSINESS PLAN

Think Through your Business Plan

Anshuman Sharma

Copyright ©2012 Anshuman Sharma

All Rights Reserved

Dedication

To my beautiful daughters Anushka and Prashansa

To my lovely wife Nilam Pathak

CONTENTS

INTRODUCTION	10
BUSINESS PLAN - STRUCTURE	14
EXECUTIVE SUMMARY	16
THE FINANCING PROPOSAL	17
Financing Proposal	18
Definitions	18
THE BUSINESS DESCRIPTION	19
The Business Description	20
Business Description	21
Offering	23
Market	26
Target Customer Segment	27
Major Events	30
Company's Future	31
Business Operations	33
Team	36
Current Financials	38
Financial Position	40
Success of the Company	45
Mission	48
Industry Classification	51
Primary Products and Service	58

- Major Companies 61
- Competitors 64
- Industry Lifecycle 69
- Sales and Revenue Growth 71
- Growth of Industry 73
- Strategic Opportunities 74
- Competitor's Offerings 75
- Our Market 77
- Special Characteristics of our Market 79
- Our Offering's Uniqueness 81
- Target Market's Purchasing Power 82
- Sales Estimates 83
- Evidence for Sales Estimates 84
- OPERATIONS 84
- Product Line 84
- Competitive Advantage 87
- Production Process 89
- SUPPORT 94
- Keys to success in Production 94
- Competitive Advantage of Production Process 95
- Services 97
- Merchandising Category 99
- Competitive Advantage of Products 100
- Selling Strategy 101

Company's Physical Facilities 104

Purchasing 105

Inventory Management 107

Quality Control 108

Customer Service 109

Personnel 110

Financing Profile 111

OPERATING PLANS 113

    INDUSTRY ANALYSIS 114

    New Entrants 114

    New offerings and innovations 116

    Technological Obsolescence 118

    Technological Changes 120

    Supply Chain 121

    Suppliers 122

    Distribution Channel 123

    Scope of Market 125

    Primary Customers 126

    Influence on Customers 127

    Factors Influencing the Industry 129

    Trends of Factors Influencing the Industry 131

    Present Behavior of the Factors Influencing the Industry ... 132

    Past Performance of Industry 133

    Industry Forecast 134

- Assumptions of Forecast 135
- Strategic Opportunity in Industry 136
- Strategic Opportunity for Us 138
- MARKET ANALYSIS AND SALES FORECAST 139
  - Market 140
  - Market Demographics 142
  - Key Factors of Market 142
  - Market Outlook 144
  - Niche Market 145
  - Target Market Segment 146
  - Our Strength in the Market 147
  - Revenues from Niche 149
  - Competitors 150
- MARKETING PLAN 151
  - Company's Philosophy 152
  - Opportunity in Market 153
  - Factors Influencing Sales 156
  - Opportunity for Niche Market 157
  - Our Consumers 159
  - Consumer Perception 161
  - Existing Market 163
  - Competitor's Image 165
  - Advertising Techniques 167
  - Pricing 170

- Competitor's SWOT 172
- Competitive Advantage 174
- Competitor's Distribution 175
- Distribution Channels 176
- Market Connection 178
- Marketing Mix 179
- Marketing Program 180
- Marketing Strategy Analysis 181
- Revenue Targets 184
- Promotional Strategy 185

THE OPERATING PLAN 186
- Value Proposition 187
- Location 188
- Operations Plan - Manufacturing 190
- Operations Plan - Services 192
- Operation Design 193
- Purchasing 195
- Inventory Management 197
- Quality Control 199

ORGANIZATION PLAN 201
- Management philosophy 202
- Organization structure 205
- Compensation and Incentives 207

THE FINANCIAL PLAN 209

Financing Summary 210

Costing 211

Costs Heads 216

Costs Assumptions 217

Revenues 219

Revenue Assumptions 222

Profits & Loss 224

Balance Sheet 227

Cash Flow 229

Valuation 231

About Author 234

INTRODUCTION

As an entrepreneur and investor, I have the privilege to develop plans for taking our existing businesses forward or to work with a team of entrepreneurs on a new solution. As a mentor and investor I also review business plans regularly of other teams who either are looking for guidance or funding. Most of these plans are for commercializing new ideas and develop them into profitable businesses. These ideas vary from technology solutions to manufacturing to services. These are developed by well educated, knowledgeable and enthusiastic people who identify an unmet need of the market and create a product or service to meet that need. This need gap must be profitable, which means that the target audience should be ready to pay for the offering to make the proposed business profitable. Many times these ideas are 'inspired' by some successful companies located in other regions or countries, a successful idea in USA like group buying can find many clones in Asian countries. These entrepreneurs also have the benefit of showing the success of the proposed model to the investors, thereby reducing overall risk. The logic of this reasoning lies in the view that a successful business model of one market can be replicated to any other market with high probability of success. This is the reason that any successful service leads to the creation of several replicas.

I am always amazed to see the quality of business plans presented to me and my team. They are poorly written. The basic structure and guidelines to develop a business plan are available all over Internet and hundreds of books are written on it. Some companies even offer specialized software to develop it. Market is abundant with consultants who offer their services to develop the business plans for these entrepreneurs. On academic front almost all management institutes and several technical institutes offer the course in entrepreneurship, which has 'business plan development' as one of the subject. People can easily obtain data and information about their industries and sectors and can conduct an in-depth research on competitors, market and customers. Even with the sea of information and support available for every potential entrepreneur, somehow, the right business plan is not created.

The reasons range from getting the right guidelines to doing proper research to putting genuine efforts in creating the business plan. For some people it could be a waste of time as they are interested in immediate action, others are not completely clear about their offerings. Some are afraid to face the reality while few get stuck at writing the plan. A weak business plan is the beginning to an end of commercializing the idea.

Looking at all these problems the plan of writing this book was conceived. The books which are available in the market are either too deep or too shallow. Most covers the description of each segment of the business plan, in detail. They even provide the business & management concepts required to analyze the company, industry and market. Some books present the sample business plans, covering fictional companies in various sectors. A segment of books focus on the tricks to raising money through astute business plans while others presents dos and don'ts. All these books may have their niche in the market and readers may look for different resources for problems encountered during the process of writing a business plan.

I found a need in the market for would-be entrepreneurs who require a resource which is simple, short and to-the-point for creating a business plan. It should guide the entrepreneur at every stage of the process, while focusing on the startups. It should be able to help even the first time entrepreneurs. The most important activity in developing a business plan is to think through each point of potential business in depth then based upon that knowledge and information create a perfect write-up about the topic which would answer most of the queries of the reader. This book would help you by taking you through that process of thinking and writing.

This resource would act as an indispensable resource for the entrepreneurs who have an idea and are looking forward to raise funds to start a company of their own. This would guide them in filling the gaps to have a complete clarity about their offering.

The aim of convincing a potential investor through a business plan is secondary; the primary objective is to build a belief about the idea. During the process of developing a business plan you tend to explore almost all aspects of the proposed business. You need to search for the information and responses to the queries and objections raised during the process. Areas for which information is not available, you need to identify some logical assumptions using common sense, information and market models available. By the end of the process you are supposed to have visited every corner of the proposed venture. The weak idea would be rejected during the business plan development process, as either it would be a loss making proposition or it leads to unsustainable profits or looks illogical. Once you are convinced with the business idea and believe in it then it is much easier to convince the investors or other potential stakeholders.

This book would provide you those guidelines to prepare a complete business plan. These guidelines would focus your energies onto the gaps to be filled, which you would do either by searching for more information or intensifying the depth of your discussions with your team. The material is organized in such a way that it would make you think through almost all aspects of your planned business.

This book would only act a support system during your process of business plan development, while the major work would be undertaken by you and your team. It can point to the weak links and gaps but the responsibility of clarifying it would rest on your shoulders. If you want you can avoid certain complex issues, which you are not able to answer, but you need to understand that they would come back to you later in much fiercer form. It would be better that all complex issues receive your special attention.

This book would take you to every section and subsection of the business plan and guide your focus onto the issues to be discussed and detailed in the document.

BUSINESS PLAN - STRUCTURE

Cover Letter

Business Plan Cover Page

Contents of the Business Plan

Summary of Financial Requirements

Executive Summary

- Business idea and purpose
- Operating plan summary
- Marketing plan summary
- Organizational plan summary
- Financial plan summary

Operating Plan

- Description of company's Location
- Description of company's operations
- Description of company layout and facilities
- Description of purchasing and distribution management
- Description of Inventory management and control system
- Description of quality control and customer service

Industry Analysis

- Description of company's industry

- Description about company's competition
- Description of industry growth and sales projections

Market Analysis

- Description about target market
- Description about company's market
- Forecast of company's sales

Financial Plan

- Description of past financial performance
- Financial projection of company

EXECUTIVE SUMMARY

Specify the following points in executive summary:

1. The concept and mission of business and reasons for its projected success
2. Brief description of product and service of business
3. Brief description of market
4. Brief description of business operations
5. Brief specification of marketing plan
6. Financial plan summary

Points for Discussion

1. What is company's basic business?
2. How business is conducted? What are the plans for future?
3. What is the market of the company's products and services?
4. What is the sales potential of the market?
5. How this market will be penetrated?
6. What is the marketing strategy of the company?
7. How company will beat the competition?
8. What is the competitive advantage of the company?
9. What is the amount of financing needed to implement the business plan?
10. What are the reasons for this amount of financing?

THE FINANCING PROPOSAL

Financing Proposal

1. What are our projected costs and revenues?
2. What is our financing requirement?
3. How this amount would be used?
4. What would be the type of financing required (debt or equity)?
5. What would be the maturity of financing required?
6. What is the valuation of the company (for equity)?
7. How much equity are we ready to dilute (for equity)?
8. What would be the payment schedule (for debt)?
9. What is available collateral (for debt)?
10. What is the present ownership structure of the company?
11. What is owners' investment?

Definitions

- For the purpose of writing we would specify "offerings" for any product, service or solution.
- 'We' and 'our' means the team developing the business plan.
- 'Startup' means a running business or company in early stages of its life or a business yet to start.

THE BUSINESS DESCRIPTION

The Business Description

Points for Discussion

1. What the investor is looking for in our business plan? What other readers would be interested in?
2. What would leave a good impression on reader about the proposed business? What would delight her?
3. What could leave a bad impression on reader about our business plan? What could bore her? What could irritate her? What could make her feel about our insincerity?
4. What can create confusion in reader's mind and what steps should we take to be crystal clear about our ideas and presentation?
5. Are all the ideas presented in the plan are in sync with each other or is there any inconsistency?
6. What are the points of contradiction and conflict and are we prepared to logically prove them?
7. Are all ideas, activities and actions presented are legal, ethical and moral?

Business Description

Specify the business which the company or the proposed venture would perform. This could be manufacturing of a product demanded in the market or a service filling a gap in the market. You should also describe the gap or demand of the market and logical reasons for it. Also attach some supporting document in the appendix, with a link (or page number) provided in this section. This section would clearly inform the reader about the business of the company.

Points for Discussion

1. Clearly and simply describe the business in minimum number of words. Any person should be able to answer "What we do" after listening to this description.
2. Clearly specify what we do not do. This is required as reader may get confused with any overlapping offerings in the market.
3. How this idea came to our mind and what need and gap our offering is trying to fill in the market?
4. What are our capabilities which make us confident for getting success in this business?
5. How are we unique to get the competitive advantage in the market?
6. What we do? How do we serve the market?
7. What values we stand for? What are those right actions, which can always be expected from us?
8. What is our mission? What is the purpose for which our business exists?
9. What is our organizational vision? How are we going to achieve our mission and purpose of existence?
10. What is our organizational culture defined by our corporate values?

11. How our organizational vision defines our organizational goals, objectives and milestones?

Offering

Specify the proposed product, service or solution of the venture. You need to specify the details of this offering and the logic to prove that it is rightly suited to fill the gap specified. Its uniqueness should also be mentioned and its reasons for success in the market.

Points for Discussion

1. What is the product we are proposing for the market?
2. What is the service we are proposing for the market? Is it a separate service or bundled with a product or solution?
3. What solution are we presenting to solve a problem in the market? This problem should be acute enough to create a profitable demand.
4. Is our offering optimally featured? Is it over-featured or under-featured?
5. What is the description of our offering? How would it satisfy the demand in the market?
6. What this offering of our company will not do?
7. Which are the segments of customer which it will not serve? Clarity is required in case of overlapping segments.
8. Why are we targeting this customer segment?
9. Why are we not targeting any other profitable segment?
10. How can we say with surety that this offering will satisfy the need of the market?
11. Why any other offering cannot satisfy the market need?
12. What are the unique and great things about our offering?

13. How does this product looks physically? Will it be appreciated by market? Could it look better and more user friendly?
14. What is the customer experience of our offering? How do they rate it? Is it above or below industry average?
15. Who are the end users of our offering?
16. What is the experience of our offering? How do consumers rate it? Is it above or below the industry experience?
17. What is the channel through which it reaches the customers? Is it the best possible channel? Can we improve it?
18. How it reaches the consumers? What is the process involved?
19. How can this offering keep improving? Are required systems in place for that?
20. Is the offering satisfactory enough to make customers pay for it?
21. Will they be our repeat customers?
22. What is the expected percentage of repeat customers from our total existing customers?
23. What is the expected duration of our offering life cycle?
24. How can this offering will keep reinventing itself with the market trends?
25. Is the demand of our offering strong in the market? Is it robust enough for normal economic, political, demographic and social factors?
26. What is the sensitivity analysis?
27. Do we still have any unresolved problem with offering?
28. If yes, how can we resolve it?
29. What are the basic risks attached with the offering?
30. What are our plans to mitigate these basic risks?
31. Can some minor changes in our offering increase the size of our target customer segment?

32. What is cost-benefit-analysis of updating our offering?
33. Will this enhancement in offering improve revenues, market share and profitability?
34. If yes, then how can we go ahead with this offering enhancement?

Market

Specify the market for the product or service. Describe how it is rightly suited for our offerings and the reasons we would be able to get success in this market.

Points for Discussion

1. Where is market geographically located?
2. Specify all the constituents of the market.
3. Who are the major players of the market?
4. How they influence the market?
5. Why are they considered the major players?
6. Why other constituents do not have much influence?
7. What are the good and positive points about this market?
8. What are the bad and negative points about this market?
9. Is market categorized as strong, average or weak by experts?
10. What are the reasons for this categorization?
11. What is the size of the market in terms of potential number of buyers?
12. What is the size of the market in terms of potential revenues?
13. How fast the market would grow in next five years?
14. What are the reasons for its growth?
15. How sensitive is the market to major factors?
16. What is the responsiveness of the market e.g. how would it behave during festivals and other events?
17. What are the major problems with this market, which may or may not affect us?
18. What the main risks related to market?
19. How can they be managed?

Target Customer Segment

Describe the target market of the product or service. Specify the customers and consumers of our offerings and the need satisfied by its usage or consumption. Describe the compelling reasons that customers would buy from our company.

Points for Discussion

1. What is the target customer segment of our offering?
2. Where is this segment located? Can we clearly identity the location of this segment? What are its other geographical factors?
3. How can this target segment be described?
4. How much they earn?
5. What are their major components of expenditure?
6. What are their other demographic factors (age, income, education, size, density, location, gender, race, occupation and other statistics)?
7. What are the main psychographic factors (Social classes, lifestyles) of this segment?
8. What are main Behavioral factors of this target customer segment (Purchase occasions, benefits sought and usage rates)?
9. How can we say that our offering would be liked and purchased by this segment?
10. What is the main gap in the market which our offering is filling?
11. What is their paying capacity?
12. What maximum amount they are ready to pay for our offering?
13. What can be most optimum pricing level for our offering to get maximum profitability and revenues?

14. How pricing affects this segment?
15. What are the substitutes of our offering available for customers?
16. What are the historical facts of this segment about using the product line of our offering?
17. What are the major problems related to this customer segment?
18. What are the risks associated with this customer segment?
19. How these risks would be managed?
20. What are the buying patterns of our potential customers?
21. What are their major dislikes in existing offerings?
22. What they appreciate and like about the existing offerings?
23. What are the main factors on which they react?
24. Who are the decision makers in this customer segment?
25. Who are the end users of our offerings?
26. How our offerings are used?
27. What is the useful life of our offering?
28. What is the time duration after which they demand upgrade of our offering?
29. What are the major factors of customer segment which are expected to change in next three years?
30. How would our offering would evolve to meet this change?
31. What is the best way to connect with them?
32. How our offering can be distributed to customers?
33. How feedback about our offering is taken from customers?
34. What are the different ways to delight them?
35. What could be major mistakes from our organization which could damage our brand image and reputation?
36. What are the other geographical locations where we can find out target customer segment?

37. Are these customer segments at other geographical locations would be profitable for us?
38. What is the cost – benefit – analysis for these segments?

Major Events

How our company has reached the current life cycle stage? Describe the major events and factors which are responsible for bringing our company to the present life cycle stage?

<u>Points for Discussion</u>

1. What is the lifecycle stage of the industry?
2. What are the advantages and disadvantages of this stage for us?
3. What is the life cycle stage of our offering?
4. What are the advantages and disadvantages of this stage for us?
5. If our understanding about the lifecycle stage is wrong, then how would it affect us?
6. What are our plans for that?

Company's Future

Define our predictions about the future of the company and our various plans to navigate our company to this future.

Points for Discussion

1. How our company is performing in the market?
2. What have been major reasons for this performance?
3. How is it in comparison to other companies in our industry?
4. What is our strategy for growth?
5. What is our execution plan for this strategy?
6. Is this strategy in sync with our mission?
7. How we would be positioned in the industry 3, 5 and 10 years from now?
8. What is our prediction about the future of industry and market?
9. What are the predictions of other players of industry about market growth?
10. Is ours a better prediction than other players in the industry?
11. How would it give us edge?
12. What is the logical reasoning to prove this prediction?
13. How much surety we have about this prediction?
14. If this prediction is proved wrong then how would it affect us?
15. Are we prepared to face these eventualities?
16. How our team is rightly placed to take our company to future success?
17. What improvements we need in our team to get this success?
18. What are our plans to get those improvements?

19. What are our contingency plans if our team is unable to perform at the required level?
20. How would we manage the unexpected rapid changes in the market?
21. How the current life cycle stage of the industry and offering would affect our business?
22. As per our future plan what is the minimum growth level which must be achieved every year?
23. What are the key factors which would support us in achieving this growth level?
24. What are the risks associated with this plan?
25. How can we manage these risks?
26. What are the major assumptions in our future plan?
27. What is the probability of each of these assumptions?
28. Are these assumptions reasonable? How are they compared with the assumptions of other players in the industry?
29. Is our plan robust? How sensitive is it to changes in assumptions and other factors?
30. Which are the crucial resources that would be required to follow the designed plan?
31. Are we working towards to procure and manage those resources?
32. Is any of our action, in anyway, going against this plan?

Business Operations

Describe the operations of our business and the reasons for these being productive and agile.

Points for Discussion

1. What are the operational facts of business?
2. Why our business operations would work, as expected?
3. What are the problems which can arise in operations?
4. What are the risks associated with operations of business?
5. How can we manage those risks?
6. What are the key success factors for required business operations?
7. What are the macro and micro productivity levels required for business activities?
8. How would we manage these required productivity levels?
9. What technology is used in our operations?
10. How is it compared with the industry standards of technology?
11. Are we using any latest technology?
12. How can operations be one of the competitive advantage for our business?
13. What are the skills and competencies required at various levels to manage operations?
14. What are our plan to fill any skills and competency gap?
15. Where can we find the skilled operations manpower?
16. Would our location help us in sourcing required manpower?

17. How would our operational cost be affected with any change in market demand?
18. Are we operationally equipped to meet the pace of the market changes?
19. Can we manage operations with increase or decrease in demand?
20. Who are the main people in operations?
21. Do we have clearly specified responsibilities for every position, without any overlapping?
22. Are operational personnel clear about their responsibilities?
23. Who are the main decision makers in operations?
24. How fast the information flows in operations?
25. How fast the decisions are implemented?
26. How are results and output monitored?
27. Are our systems efficient enough to identify any resistance or problem in operational flow?
28. What are the operational facts of industry?
29. How is our operational performance in comparison with industry?
30. What are the operational best practices of our industry?
31. Can we learn something about best operational practices from other industries, which would help us to lead our industry in operations?
32. How can we describe our supply chain?
33. How efficient is it in comparison to industry?
34. How our supply chain management is better than other players?
35. Are we following the best practices and processes of Supply Chan Management (SCM)?
36. What are the main processes of our supply chain?
37. How do we make sure that they remain efficient?
38. How our supply chain was designed?
39. Who were the people involved in design of supply chain and its strategy?

40. Can we have the better design of the supply chain? Can other markets and industries give us ideas?
41. What major statistical tools are we using to manage the productivity of supply chain?
42. Can we find new and better ways to manage the productivity of our supply chain?

Team

Describe the management team of our business. We need to describe the reasons for our confidence on this team and their abilities to grow this business.

<u>Points for Discussion</u>

1. Who are the people in management team?
2. Why are they right people for managing this company?
3. What are strengths and weaknesses of each?
4. How would their weaknesses affect the company?
5. How as a team they support each other by complimenting each other?
6. What is the basic management structure of the company?
7. Who are the strategic decisions makers and how is the decision taken?
8. Is the decision making fast and efficient? How can we say that?
9. What could be the reasons which can reduce the effectiveness of these strategic decisions?
10. How can we face these reasons which affect the decision making process?
11. Have we checked this process of making decisions and their effectiveness with some simulations?
12. What all scenario analysis we have done to check the decision making process at various managerial levels?
13. How the resignation of a crucial manager or executive would affect the functioning of the company?
14. How can we manage this event of resignation of a crucial manager or executive?

15. What is the process to hire a capable person for vacant managerial position?
16. How fast can we do these crucial hiring?
17. What would be the cost incurred by the company for this process?
18. Can this cost be reduced in any way?
19. How industry players face this problem? What cost they incur? Can we learn anything from them?
20. What is the cost to company to maintain the team of top management?
21. What are the major components of this cost? What is the ratio of fixed and variable cost?
22. How is this cost of management executives in comparison to other personnel costs?
23. How is this cost in comparison to industry average?
24. In what ways can this cost be reduced?
25. Have we clearly defined the KRAs (Key Result Areas) for each manager?
26. How would these KRAs be quantified to measure the performance of each top manager?
27. What are the advantages and disadvantages of this type of measurement of performance?
28. How industry measures the performance of the top management?
29. Who are the key people supporting the top management to perform their day to day duties?
30. What are the major reasons for the existing management structure of our company?
31. What is the percentage of top managers leaving the company every year? How is this percentage in comparison to industry average?
32. What are the main points which prove the commitment and passion for the proposed business?
33. If some person from the founding team breaks this trust then how would they be punished?

Current Financials

Describe the current financials of the company. We need to describe the growth of company's financial over time and the reasons for our optimism for our financial success.

Points for Discussion

1. What is the current financial position of the company?
2. Where are we standing in comparison to other players in the industry?
3. What right or wrong we have done to reach the current financial status?
4. Could it be worse than present level? Why?
5. What we could have done to be in a much stronger position?
6. According to our past plan, where have we reached?
7. According to our past plan, what is remaining? What are the reasons for that?
8. What actions are we going to take to achieve this planned position?
9. What strengths and skills are required to reach this planned position?
10. Do we have the required skills and strengths? Where is the gap?
11. What is required to build these skills and strengths?
12. What are the reasons that we were not able to fill the gap?
13. How are we planning to fill this gap?
14. Where we have reached till now?
15. How our life will change for better if we achieve the required financial position?
16. How our team's personal life will be affected with this financial position?

17. What are the problems?
18. What would be the solutions to specified problems?
19. How similar activities were done in the past or by other players?

Financial Position

Describe our financial position in the industry and the reasons that the current financial position would improve in future.

Points for Discussion

1. Financially, how would our company place itself in industry?
2. Which are the financially strongest and weakest companies in the industry?
3. Is present financial position respectable in relation to the life of the company?
4. What the reasons which has placed us in the stronger financial position?
5. What are the reasons which are keeping us in weaker position? What activities can take us to the stronger position?
6. What were the wrong decisions which created resistance for our financial growth?
7. Which decisions were right? What can we learn from them?
8. What is the gap between "Where we have reached" and "Where we should have been"?
9. What we need to do to fill this gap?
10. How can we make sure that similar gaps do not exist in the future?
11. If we do not reach the desired financial level then what should be the punishment? Who would take the responsibility of this lag?
12. If we reach only a part of this level then what would be our actions?
13. How would investors react to it?
14. How would we bridge the gap in funds?
15. Would we take debt or in some other way?

16. How would we raise the funds for expansion?
17. Will it be debt or equity or mix of both?
18. What would be the reasons for this decision?
19. What would be the process of raising funds through debt?
20. What would be the process of raising funds through equity?
21. How should we prepare ourselves for this event?
22. What is the valuation of our company?
23. How this valuation is calculated?
24. What is the valuation of our brand? How is this calculated?
25. What is the valuation of the company using different valuation techniques? How are these techniques different? What is the valuation of our company with each valuation technique?
26. What would be the best suitable method for valuing our company? This method should be acceptable in the market.
27. Do we have any other company with similar business model in our industry or any other market, which is valued by the market and can act as a reference for valuation?
28. If none of similar company exist then what should be our reference for valuing our company?
29. If our company valuation calculated without any reference then what ways can this valuation be proved wrong?
30. If our company does not own high value assets then how would the valuation of our company be calculated?
31. How investors rate us on risk scale? Why? How this rating would affect us while raising funds for the company and calculating valuation of the company?
32. For equity based fund raising what is the minimum valuation we can agree with? What are the reasons for this valuation?

33. For equity based funding what is the maximum percentage of equity are we ready to dilute? What are the reasons for this figure?
34. If potential investor insist on more equity and control then what would be our stand?
35. If investor insists on bringing in other investors then how would we take it forward?
36. If the investor demands more control in board of the company, then how would we manage it and what would be our stand?
37. If investor tries to force us to accept extremely tight agreement then how would we manage it?
38. If funds release (for business operations) becomes contingent to many conditions in agreement with investors, then would we accept it?
39. If funds are released month by month then what would be our stand on that?
40. If investor demands the complete control of the financials of the company, then what would be acceptable and unacceptable to us?
41. If investors demand more control in strategic decision making, would we accept it?
42. If investors demand more control in day to day operations, through their representatives, then what would be our stand on that?
43. For reporting, if we are asked by investors to report daily activities to their representatives then how would we take it?
44. If majority stake is demanded in our company by potential investors, then would it acceptable to us? Why?
45. What are the various exit strategies for investors in our industry?
46. Which exit strategies of investors would be acceptable to us? Why?
47. Which exit strategies of investors would not be acceptable to us? Why?

48. If required, what would be our exit strategy from the company? What conditions need to be fulfilled for this decision?
49. What we need to be careful about if we exit the company? This would help us to take right decisions while signing the agreement with investors.
50. How the control would be transferred to the next management?
51. If shareholder agreement's clauses and conditions are not mutual then would we agree to them?
52. Due to some reasons if investors stop funding us midway, then how would we manage the operations of the company?
53. If a deadline of self-funding is set by board, then how would we manage it?
54. If investors put the liability of money lost in business (if things go bad and we could not make money in business) on us, then would it be acceptable to us?
55. How the reporting (maybe daily, weekly or monthly) to inventors would be managed?
56. Investors puts several stringent conditions (like "you cannot enter the industry or similar industries for next five years") in agreement, will it be acceptable to us?
57. If amount of investor's investment is dependent on the amount of founder's investment, then how would we manage it? What would be that amount? Why?
58. If total amount raised falls short of required amount then what would be our next steps?
59. Can funds raised from investors contain the component of debt?
60. In what way can we prove our team's commitment to the venture? Investors may demand some type of surety for commitment, how can we manage that?
61. How many investors rejected funding to us? What were the reasons? Do we have convincing answers to those now?

62. Are we prepared to face the strong logic presented by investors against our idea, offerings and company?

Success of the Company

Describe the reasons for our confidence for the success of our company. Specify the uniqueness we offer to the market which improves our chances of success.

Points for Discussion

1. Are we confident this company will be successful?
2. What is our confidence level?
3. What are the reasons and facts which give us this confidence?
4. What are our strategies and plans for the growth of the company, its revenues and profitability?
5. How are they different from the main industry players?
6. How can we say that our plans are correct and better than others?
7. What are the main requirements for this strategy implementation?
8. What are the major constraints in strategy implementation?
9. What is our main action plan which gives us surety of success?
10. How would this action plan be implemented?
11. What is the uniqueness of this plan?
12. How is this different from other players in the market?
13. How fast they would be able to copy it?
14. How can we manage our existing edge in the market?
15. What are our company-wide limitations (specify all) for getting success?
16. Which are major limitations for getting required growth?

17. How does each limitation affect us? What are the solutions? How can they be implemented?
18. Who among the founding team would take the moral responsibility for any failure in business?
19. If required revenue and profitability targets are not achieved then what should be the penalty for top management?
20. If required revenue and profitability targets are achieved then what should be the reward for the team?
21. What are main assumptions about various internal and external factors, based on which our plans and strategies are created?
22. How any wrong assumption would affect us?
23. Are our plans and strategy flexible but robust enough to endure any variation in assumptions?
24. When and how that changes in plans and strategy would come?
25. Are we missing some facts for predicting and designing the success of our company?
26. Do we have some examples and cases of successful companies which used similar plans and strategies?
27. Is it possible that the strategy which worked for those successful companies may not work for us?
28. Can we identify some failed companies with similar plans and strategy? What were the main reasons for their failure? What can we learn from their experiences?
29. What are the risks?
30. How those risks can be managed? Are these risk management techniques among the best?
31. Are we prepared to manage those risks?
32. Is it possible that we missed to consider some risks?
33. How this risk management process is in comparison with industry standards?
34. Can investors and other major stakeholders, in any way, doubt our skills set?

35. Can investors and other major stakeholders, in any way, doubt our honesty and intensions?
36. Have we considered most scenarios to test our plans and strategy?
37. In what ways can someone raise questions on our assumptions? Are we prepared to face those?
38. Is our team complete in skill-set and competencies to manage the company for desired growth? If not, what are our plans to fill the skill and competency gap?
39. Do we have any uniqueness about our marketing for better impact in marekt? Why is it unique?
40. How confident are we about the desired impact produced by our marketing?
41. Can someone prove our market analysis wrong? How are we going to face those questions?
42. How are our selling and distribution costs in comparison to industry standards? How do we plan to reduce those costs without affecting productivity?
43. How can we maintain the regular flow of innovative ideas?
44. How are we going to manage and use those ideas to improve ourselves regularly?
45. How would we maintain the high level of customer satisfaction? How can we better than other industry players to keep this level high?
46. How can we delight our customers?
47. Does our team have credentials and experience to drive our company on successful path?
48. If in some way we are slipped out of right path, how would we bring ourselves on the path of success?
49. Have we conducted sensitivity analysis on the factors of success?

Mission

Describe the mission statement of our company. Describe the reasons for this mission and its link with company's strategy and goals.

Points for Discussion

1. What is the mission of our company? What is the meaning of our mission?
2. Why do we have this mission for our company?
3. How our products and services linked to our mission?
4. Can this mission be interpreted in any other way? If it can be interpreted in any other way then it would create confusion about the purpose of the existence of the company.
5. Is our mission defined in way that sends similar message to all stakeholders? If there is any discrepancy in message received, how can we solve it?
6. How our various functions of company are in sync with our mission? Functions like sales, marketing, human resource, support, finance etc. are guided by corporate mission.
7. What is our strategy which is in sync with our mission?
8. What is our vision? How is it linked to our mission?
9. What are our short term objectives and goals? How is it linked to our mission?
10. What internal events may impact our commitment to our mission? What actions do we need to take to keep our commitment to our mission?
11. What external events may impact our commitment to our mission? What actions do we need to take to keep our commitment to our mission?

12. What gaps we need to fill in our strategy to keep our commitment to our mission, without getting disturbed by any external or internal events?
13. What we need to do to communicate our mission to all our stakeholders?
14. Have we defined the expected actions, responsibilities and expected output for each position in the company, in accordance with the mission?
15. Do we measure the performance of each personnel based upon the above definition?
16. How do we ensure that all stakeholder actions are in sync with our mission?
17. How does the clarity of mission affect our marketing and sales strategy?
18. How does the clarity of mission affect our financial strategy and accounting practices?
19. How does the clarity of mission affect our human resource management and operational practices?
20. How do we ensure that the decisions taken in our company, at every level, are in accordance with our mission?
21. How does the clarity of our mission ease our decision making process?
22. How can we make sure that our execution is among the best in industry? How our clarity of mission supports it?
23. How our mission is related to CSR (Corporate Social Responsibility)? How does it define the actions for us?
24. How our corporate brand image reflects our mission? If our brand image does not clearly delivers the message of mission, then what we need to do to bring that clarity?
25. Can we identify any company which can act a role model for our company?

26. What is the mission of this role-model company? How is it compared to ours?
27. What are values of our company which guide us to follow our mission?
28. What is the culture of our company? How does it make us behave in right way to achieve our mission?

Industry Classification

Describe our industry and its classification. Specify our confidence on the growth of industry and the reasons associated with it.

Points for Discussion

1. What is the classification of our industry and sector?
2. Our industry is categorized in which department or ministry of government?
3. What are the government standards for this industry?
4. How is this industry rated in terms of growth, profitability, importance and other parameters in comparison to other industries?
5. Do the offerings of this industry overlap with any other industry? How does that affect us?
6. What we need to do to manage any problem arising out of this overlapping?
7. How is this industry controlled and managed by government? How many government authorities are involved in it – federal, state and local?
8. How is industry regulated?
9. Are its offerings regulated by other regulators?
10. How does the overlapping of regulators affects our business? What we need to do to manage it?
11. Are the regulations imposed by government regulators stringent? What can we do about it? What can we do about to manage our business profitable even with these regulations?
12. How does government policy and legal rules affect us? What steps should we take to get advantage out of these policies?
13. How industry has responded to these regulations, policies and rules?

14. What are the good points related to our industry? How are we taking advantage from these strengths of our industry?
15. What are the bad points related to our industry? How can we protect ourselves from these weaknesses of our industry?
16. What support has been provided by government for this industry? What advantage have we taken from the support provided by government?
17. What is the role of foreign companies in our industry? How their actions affect us?
18. What is the import and export policy of government for our industry? What are the good and bad points of it? How does it affect us? What should be our international strategy to take full advantage of this policy?
19. What is tax structure and policy for our industry and our offerings? How is it in comparison to other offerings and industries?
20. How tax policies of government affect us? How can we manage it to take the maximum advantage?
21. What is expected tax policy of government for next three to five years? How this information would help us to design our strategy and take decisions for taking full advantage of tax policy?
22. What is the supply chain of our industry? Who are players of this chain? Which are the main players of supply chain?
23. What is the financial standing of the main players of supply chain? How does this affects their performance?
24. What is the raw material of industry?
25. What is the raw material for our offerings?
26. How is it sourced?
27. Which are the major suppliers of raw materials in our industry?
28. What is the influence and bargaining power of these suppliers in our industry?

29. What is the value chain of the industry? Where are we placed in it?
30. Is our supply chain efficient? What are the reasons for this efficiency?
31. How do the efficiency levels of supply chain affect us? What steps do we need to take to maintain our productivity levels?
32. What are the major factors which affect this industry?
33. How are these factors related to other industries and sectors?
34. How do these factors affect us? How can we minimize the effects of these factors so that we have major control on our business?
35. How national and international economic conditions affect us?
36. Which economic indicators affect our industry most? Understand the meaning and trend of each.
37. How other economic factors affect our industry? How would it help us to design our future plans?
38. What is our economic forecast for next three to five years? How would these economic trends affect us? What we need to do to use these economic trends to improve our revenues and profitability in comparison to other industry players?
39. What are the risks which affect our industry maximum? Describe each of them.
40. Which are major risks? How these risks affect us? What can we do to mitigate them?
41. How the tax policies of government affect the buying behavior of our customers?
42. How other social factors affect the sales of our products? What we need to do to manage our business among these factors?
43. How many business associations are present in our industry? In what ways are they helping our industry? What can we do to use the power of these associations to help industry and our company?

44. How is the labor and worker supply in our industry? How does it affect us?
45. What is our strategy to meet any labor, worker or skills shortage?
46. Which labor unions are active in our industry? What type of activism these unions get involved? How does it affect us?
47. What are the major demands of these labor unions? How would we face the challenges posed by these unions?
48. How would we define the technology of the industry? How complex is this technology?
49. Can technology be a competitive advantage for our industry?
50. Which is the latest technology associated with our industry?
51. Can we identify any disruptive technology in the pipeline? How disruptive technology affected our industry in the past?
52. How do we rate ourselves in technology usage in our industry?
53. What are our plans to use technology to increase our revenues and reduce our costs?
54. How fast the technology changes in our industry? What are the main reasons for the speed of this change?
55. How does this change affects us? How does it affect other players of the industry?
56. Who are the main suppliers of technology to industry?
57. How the technology has evolved for our industry? How is it predicted to change in future?
58. What is our technology strategy to take the maximum advantage from the evolution of technology?
59. How do we need to equip ourselves for the execution of technology strategy?
60. How the present leaders of the industry got that position? What can we learn from them?

61. What do we need to do to compete with the present leaders of the industry?
62. How the industry players arrange funds for business? What are the major sources?
63. What is the normal structure of funds raised for business?
64. How complex is it to raise money for business in our industry?
65. What is our financial strategy to raise funds for our company?
66. Have we tested our financial strategy with scenario analysis?
67. How does stock market treats our industry? Do we have companies in our industry which are performing consistently well on stock-markets? What are the reasons for their performance?
68. Which are the worst performing companies from our industry on the stock markets? What are the reasons for their low performance?
69. How our industry performs at stock-markets worldwide? How is it different from the national markets? What are the reasons for this difference?
70. How are the stock-markets expected to behave in future? How is it going to affect us our business? How are we going to face any problems of industry on stock-markets?
71. What is our plan for IPO?
72. What would be the main financial ratios of our company? What does this ratio analysis of our industry indicate?
73. What would be the analysis and reaction of investors and other experts about our company?
74. What would be the exit plan of investors from our company? When and why they would want to exit?
75. What are the historical facts of our company?
76. What are the problems of the company? How can they be solved?

77. What is the ratio analysis for the company? What is the interpretation of the ratio analysis?
78. What is the analysis of other companies of the industry?
79. What is the number of respectable players in our industry offering same or similar products?
80. Which clusters exist in our industry? How do they affect us? How can these clusters add value to us?
81. Who are the leaders of the industry? Why are they considered as leaders?
82. Who are the losers of the industry? Why are they considered as losers?
83. What strategies could industry losers use to gain stronger position in the industry?
84. Which turnaround strategy and plan could be used by weak companies of our industry to gain leadership position in the industry?
85. What is the investment for R&D in our industry? What is the expected ROI for this investment?
86. What is the amount of money which had already been invested in R&D? What type of innovations can we expect in the future in our industry?
87. What is our capacity for investment in R&D? What ROI do we expect?
88. How can R&D investment affect our future?
89. How can R&D help us in beating our competitors?
90. What are the normal inventory levels for our industry?
91. What is the cost associated with the inventory?
92. How can we manage this cost of inventory?
93. Which are the powerful companies of our industry?
94. Who are the powerful people and influencer of our industry?
95. How are we related to them? How their connection can help us in business?
96. How can we connect with them and build better relations?
97. How strong is our network in our industry?
98. What we need to do to build this network?

99. How, a person with better connections and networking in our industry would be able to manage her business better?
100. What is the basic process for building business relations in our industry?
101. What is five forces analysis of my industry?
102. What is the attrition rate of my industry and how is it compared to others?
103. What is the reason for this rate?
104. How will this attrition rate affect us?
105. Which companies have the best retention rate in our industry? How are they able to manage this rate? What can we learn from them?
106. Do students from the top institutes choose us as an option to start their career?
107. How do we pay our employees in comparison to other players of industry?
108. What is the SWOT (Strength, Weakness, Opportunity and Threats) analysis of our industry?
109. Is our industry consolidating?
110. If no, what are the reasons for that?
111. When do we expect consolidation to start in our industry?
112. How consolidation would affect us and our ability to perform business?
113. If our company is an acquisition target then will our shareholders would be interested in that or not?
114. What are the reasons for that?
115. How this decision would be taken and what factors can change that decision?

Primary Products and Service

Describe the products and services provided by the industry. Specify the projected future of these products & services and the reasons associated with these projections.

Points for Discussion

1. What are our products and services of our industry?
2. What needs and demands of the market are satisfied by our industry?
3. What market is ready to pay for our products and services?
4. What are the margins for our industry? How are these margins in comparison to other industries?
5. How our products reach customers?
6. Who are the customers and consumers of our products and services?
7. What are the major costs associated with industry?
8. Which of these costs are fixed and variable?
9. What we need to do to reduce these costs?
10. What are the key success factors for these products?
11. What are the substitute products which the market offers?
12. What is the description of each substitute product and how they satisfy market demand?
13. How do these substitute products affect our company?
14. What is our strategy to beat these substitute products?
15. How features of our offerings affect sales in market?
16. How our products and services are differentiated in the market?
17. What we need to do to differentiate our products?

18. How our products are used by consumers?
19. Do we need any supporting product or service to increase the appeal of our products?
20. How these supporting products would affect our sales?
21. How the product qualities of other industry players affect our sales?
22. What are the other competitive factors which affect the sale of our offerings?
23. How these products reach customers?
24. Which channels are used to deliver our offerings?
25. Are customers satisfied with the offerings of industry?
26. How do we take the customers feedback?
27. How do we improve our offerings?
28. What methods we use to improvise our offerings?
29. How new products and services are developed?
30. How these new offerings are tested in the market?
31. How do we perform alpha and beta testing on products?
32. What is the process of our Research and Development of products?
33. How new ideas of products and services are conceived?
34. What is the government outlook on our products and services?
35. What rules and regulations have been placed on our products?
36. How do these rules and regulations affect our functioning?
37. How do we manage our operations and marketing within the guidelines specified by the government?
38. What is the tax structure related to our industry?
39. What is the future outlook of the industry?
40. What is the life cycle for industry's products?
41. At which stage of the life cycle each product is placed?

42. How this would affect us?
43. How would we reinvent to increase the life of the product line?

Major Companies

Describe the major companies of the industry. Specify the strengths and weaknesses of these companies and their impact on our company.

Points for Discussion

1. Which are the major companies in the industry?
2. What is their financial status?
3. Why are they categorized as major companies in the industry?
4. What are the major geographical locations of the companies of the industry?
5. What are the reasons for these locations? Is it due to raw materials, favorable policies, talent or something else?
6. What is the total number of companies in the industry?
7. How many companies are performing poorly in the industry?
8. What are the reasons for these low performing companies?
9. Which companies are most profitable?
10. Which companies have biggest market share in their product category?
11. Which companies have maximum revenues?
12. Which are the companies with maximum product lines?
13. Which companies are respected in our industry?
14. Which companies people what to join in our industry?
15. What is the brand equity of each major player in the industry?
16. What is the valuation of every profitable company in the industry?
17. How is this valuation calculated?
18. How this environment of valuation would affect our valuation?

19. How this process of valuation calculation in industry would affect our company's valuation?
20. How many companies are listed in major stock exchanges?
21. How these companies are traded in stock exchanges?
22. What is the attrition rate of each company? What are the reasons for that?
23. How companies attract talent?
24. What are the industry standards for employee remuneration?
25. How do these standards affect our ability to attract talent?
26. Has any company disrupted the industry through innovation?
27. How and why this innovation was able to disrupt the industry?
28. How other companies reacted to it?
29. What is the probability of similar disruption in our industry in near future?
30. What we need to do to create disruption in industry through innovation?
31. How technology is used in our industry?
32. Which are the major technologies used in our industry?
33. Which products, services or processes get the benefit of these technologies?
34. How new technologies impacts our industry?
35. Which technologies are most productive?
36. How these technologies improve productivity?
37. What are the short-term and long-term plans of main companies of our industry?
38. What are their business strategies?
39. Which plans have worked for these companies in the past?
40. Which are the best practices of the industry?
41. Which are the major processes of the industry?
42. How productive are these processes and how can we improve them?

43. How are companies improvising on these processes?
44. Which are the major MNCs active in the industry?
45. How many foreign companies are present in our industry? What advantages and disadvantages do they have for our company?
46. How are these foreign companies affecting the environment of the industry? What good and bad are they brining to our industry?
47. What is the major strength of these foreign companies? Is it management, technology, reach, sourcing, marketing or branding?
48. What is the SWOT of each company of the industry?
49. Where do you want to reach in this industry?
50. What are milestones of your business plan?
51. What do we need to do to follow this plan successfully?
52. What resources we need to have to follow this plan?
53. What is the gap in required resources? What do we need to do to fill this gap?
54. What challenges do we have to fill this resource gap?
55. How can we meet these challenges?
56. How major companies affect our industry positively and negatively?
57. How can we face the negative influence of these companies?
58. Do we have other obstructions in industry like monopoly practices etc.? If yes, then what is our plan to face them?

Competitors

Specify the major competitors of the industry. Describe their strengths, weaknesses and strategy. Discuss the reasons of our superiority over these companies.

Points for Discussion

1. Who are our competitors?
2. How can they be categorized in size, profitability, market share and other factors?
3. What are their plans about growth?
4. What are their mission, vision and values?
5. What are their short term and long term goals?
6. Which companies are able to meet their goals and follow their corporate mission?
7. What is the business strategy of each competitor?
8. What are the reasons for this strategy?
9. How do their strategies differ?
10. What are the reasons for this difference in strategy among competitors?
11. How are these competitors performing in the market?
12. How many competitors are profitable? How many competitors are in losses?
13. What right or wrong do these profitable and loss making companies respectively are doing?
14. What is the profitability of successful companies in our industry?
15. What is the size of the losses of loss making companies in our industry?
16. What is the ratio of profitable and loss making companies?
17. Which strategies seem to work in our industry?
18. What efforts these loss making companies are taking to become profitable?
19. What are the chances of their recovery?

20. What insights, information and data are required to develop the strategy for our company?
21. How can we say that we would be profitable in this business?
22. How business strategy would help us in our growth and profitability?
23. How the strategies and actions of competitors affect each other?
24. How their strategies and actions impact us?
25. How can these companies act against us?
26. What can we do to protect ourselves?
27. How fast our competitors learn and adept?
28. How fast they copy us in offerings and techniques?
29. How can we protect our profitability?
30. What events can make the companies in industries to fight for survival?
31. How this would be fought?
32. Which type of companies would be winners in that fight?
33. What we need to do to be among those winners?
34. Do we have common or overlapping sales and distribution channels with our competitors?
35. How competitors can affect our sales and distribution channels?
36. What can we do to protect ourselves from any disruption?
37. How are we different from our competitors in terms of products, services, team, processes, marketing, sales, support etc.?
38. What is our USP (Unique Selling Proposition)?
39. What is our competitive advantage?
40. How do we offer differentiation in the market?
41. How can we create our brand?
42. How can we enhance our brand equity?
43. Which are the strong brands in our industry?
44. What is the value of these brands?
45. How are these brands evolving with time?

46. How would the existing brands affect us in building our brand?
47. What are the strong and weak points of competing brands?
48. What are the strong and weak points of our brand?
49. How can we exploit the weak points of our competing brands?
50. Are our competitors are involved in wrong and corrupt practices?
51. How can we beat them through ethical means?
52. How our future would be placed at risk if our team get involve in these unethical practices?
53. How can we make sure that our team do not involve in unethical practices?
54. How do these companies with corrupt practices deal with media and other government authorities?
55. What is the advertising expenditure of our competitors?
56. How do they advertise?
57. Which are the niches which competitors serve?
58. What other products and services do competitors offer to market?
59. How these products and services support competitors in our product line?
60. How these products and services are related to our offerings?
61. How fast these competitors update their product range which could put pressure on us?
62. How can we equip ourselves to face this challenge by offering better but required products and services to market?
63. What is our strategy to improve our offerings regularly?
64. How can competitors attract our star employees? Does industry has this type of practice?
65. What can we do to protect any hijack of our employees?
66. Can we hire our competitor's best employees?

67. How can we hire our competitor's best employees? What process do we need to follow to recruit these employees?
68. What resources do we need to have to hire best professionals of our industry?
69. Who are the main people who are driving our competitor's companies?
70. How can we build our team to beat these good managers of our competitors?
71. What can we learn from these good professionals about business management?
72. How can we implement this new learning in our company?
73. What data do we have about our competitors?
74. How can we use this data about our competitors?
75. What information can we get about our competitors?
76. How can we use this information in our plans and meeting our goals?
77. Which information is available publicly?
78. What exactly we want to know about our competitors, which can be extracted from available data and information?
79. What public information is available about us?
80. What all other information our competitors can get about us?
81. What interpretation an analyst can get about us from the data available about our company?
82. How these interpretations would affect competitor's decisions and actions?
83. How these decisions and actions of our competitor would affect us?
84. What do we need to do to be ready to face these decisions and actions of competitors?
85. What MIS (Management Information System) do our competitors use?
86. What information and insights can they get from the MIS system?

87. Which MIS system do we use?
88. What information are we generating from MIS and what insights are we able to develop?
89. How can we use this for competitive advantage?
90. How can we use the trends of the market to improve our revenues?
91. What can we do to be better at understanding trends in the market?

Industry Lifecycle

Specify the life cycle of the industry and the factors which affect it. Describe the reasons which would help us to utilize the current stage of the life cycle for improving our market share and profitability.

Points for Discussion

1. What is the lifecycle of the industry?
2. What is the time-period of each stage of the life cycle?
3. How have we calculated the time period of each stage? Do we have some empirical study proving it? How it matches with the calculations of others?
4. What is the life cycle stage of the industry?
5. What makes us sure about the current life cycle stage of our industry?
6. What are the indicators which tell us about the life cycle of the industry?
7. Do we have some previous life cycles of the industry?
8. What can we interpret from these life cycles?
9. How has the industry reinvented to break the decline of the previous life cycles?
10. Which factors would lead to stagnation of industry?
11. Which factors would pull the industry down?
12. How would we deal with the stagnation or weakness in industry?
13. How would we maintain our sales and profitability?
14. How can we take advantage of this phase of industry?
15. How can we assure others about the future success of the industry?

16. What is our prediction about the reinvention of industry after stagnation or decline? How would it reinvent in future?
17. What major factors would contribute in reinvention of our industry?
18. What is the lifecycle of each offering of the industry?
19. What is the average duration of the life cycle?
20. What is the present stage of each product of industry?
21. What is the present stage of products of our company?
22. What events or factors can disturb this life cycle of industry or products?
23. How this disturbance would affect us?
24. What can we do to take advantage of the present situation?
25. Do we have contradictory or mismatching life cycles with economic and business cycles?
26. How and why this mismatch would affect us?
27. What do we need to do to protect ourselves or use it to develop our business?
28. How can we be the force of reinvention in the industry and business cycles?
29. What are the trends which affect our predictions about life cycles?
30. How competitors and industry expert's analysis does matches with ours?
31. Why is it different?

Sales and Revenue Growth

Specify our projections about the market share and revenue growth. Describe the reason for this growth and the strategy to sustain it.

Points for Discussion

1. What is the expected rate of industry growth?
2. What are our projections for next one, three and five years?
3. What factors would lead to the growth of industry?
4. How our product line would grow?
5. What are the reasons for this prediction?
6. How our offering in that segment would grow?
7. What are the main reasons for this forecast?
8. How fast other products and services of industry would grow? Why?
9. What is our understanding from these forecasts?
10. What is the present scenario for our segment and offering?
11. What is the total sale of the segment?
12. What is our market share?
13. What factors affect the revenue growth of industry?
14. What is the meaning of each of the factors affecting the growth of industry?
15. What is the variance of these factors over a time period? What are the reasons for this variance?
16. What is the present status of these factors?
17. What are the risks associated with above mentioned factors?
18. What is our risk mitigation strategy?
19. What factors could affect our product revenues?
20. What is the meaning of each of above mentioned factors?
21. What is the variation of these factors?

22. What is the present status of these factors?
23. What are the risks associated with above mentioned factors?
24. What is our risk mitigation strategy?
25. Have we analyzed all possible unfavorable scenarios for industry and us?
26. How the situations in these scenarios affect us?
27. What actions can we take to come out of these critical situations?
28. What is the profitability of industry and our company?
29. How is our profitability in comparison to other sectors with similar product and companies from different markets?

Growth of Industry

Describe the growth of industry in relation to national and global economy. Describe the current and projected economic factors and indicators which prove the growth of industry.

Points for Discussion

1. How industry is linked to economy?
2. Which economic indicators, macro and micro, affect us?
3. What does this link, between economic indicators and our company growth, tells us about the future?
4. How can a discrepancy come to this link?
5. How would it affect our forecast?
6. Do we need to create forecasts with different logical assumptions and probabilities?
7. How can we take advantage of healthy indicators?
8. How can we deal with negative ones?
9. How our product sale is linked with the industry and broader economy?
10. What indications do we get about our revenue growth?
11. How our strategy would be affected with this information?
12. How can we utilize this information to develop better plans and equip ourselves?
13. How reliable is the team doing analysis and research?
14. Do we need to take the second opinion about the insights generated by this team?

Strategic Opportunities

Specify the strategic opportunities available in the industry and the reason for our choice of the industry. Describe the plans to utilize these opportunities to improve profitability.

Points for Discussion

1. What are our main reasons to choose this industry?
2. Which of these reasons have strategic implications?
3. Which are the other industries with similar opportunities?
4. What are the main opportunities in this industry?
5. How can we monetize these opportunities in our industry?
6. How other players are looking at these opportunities and what are their plans to monetize these opportunities?
7. How incumbents and new entrants are using these opportunities?
8. What is the investment scenario in our industry? (more opportunities means more investment)
9. How is this scenario in comparison to other industries?
10. Are we equipped to utilize these opportunities?
11. How can we utilize these opportunities?
12. Which product or service of our company can take advantage of the existing opportunity?
13. How others view this opportunity?
14. How do we see it?
15. What makes us feel that our view of opportunity is better than other players?
16. Are we prepared for the scenario when this opportunity proves to be a dud?

Competitor's Offerings

Describe our offerings (products and services) to the market and their differentiation in the market. Specify the main reasons for our projected success due to the uniqueness of our offerings.

Points for Discussion

1. How can we define our competitors?
2. Which are the competitors of our products and services?
3. Which are the substitutes of our products?
4. What is unique about our products which can develop new markets?
5. How this uniqueness about our products would be difficult to be copied by competitors and other companies?
6. What is the lead time we have to capture the market until the product has copy-cats?
7. How can we retain our differentiation even after competitors enter the market?
8. How would the differentiation in products affect the price?
9. How exactly the product is differentiated?
10. What problems can arise due to this differentiation?
11. What is our strategy to face these problems?
12. What would be our methodology to communicate the product differentiation to the market?
13. How can we be sure that this offering would be liked by the market?
14. What is the value proposition of our offering to the consumers?
15. Is the product differentiation substantial enough to make people use and pay for it?

16. What are the associated risks with our product differentiation?
17. How can we mitigate these risks?
18. How the product differentiation would affect the costs like development, storage, distribution etc.?
19. What is the cost-benefit-analysis of this differentiation?

Our Market

Define our market. Describe the fit of our products and services in this market and reasons for its success.

Points for Discussion

1. What is the geographical location of the market?
2. How this geographical location of market would affect the marketing, selling and distribution?
3. In what way would we capture the pulse of the market?
4. What are the different ways to connect to the market?
5. How this market reacts to any new product or service?
6. How has the market behaved in the past about the similar offerings launches?
7. What is our understanding about the market behavior of past launches?
8. How can we penetrate the market with new offerings?
9. What are the major challenges to penetrate the market with new offerings?
10. Who are our customers and consumers of our offerings?
11. How our customers and consumers are different?
12. What are the buying habits of the customers of our offerings?
13. How the buying habits of our offerings would support the sales of our products?
14. How and where the market would expand for our offerings?
15. How do we need to update our offering to meet the need of extended market?

16. How would we know about the changes to be brought in offerings?
17. What is the process of our testing these updated offerings for expanded markets?
18. How would we able to manage our offerings in the market?
19. What is our understanding about the change in demand?
20. How any change in demand would affect the sale of our offerings?
21. What do we need to do to keep growing without stagnating or declining?
22. How market regulations affect us?
23. What are the positive and negative points of these market regulations?
24. How can we take advantage of the positive points and protect ourselves from negative points?
25. What are our forecasts about the market?
26. What is our process to calculate the forecasts?
27. How our business strategy is suitable for these business forecasts?
28. How is our strategy flexible but robust enough to take care of any market shocks?
29. How have we tested the flexibility and robustness of our strategy?

Special Characteristics of our Market

Describe the factors of market which would contribute to the growth of our company. Specify the reasons that our company would be able to utilize these factors for our growth.

Points for Discussion

1. What were the reasons for us to choose the particular geographical location for business?
2. Which reasons are making this location unique for business?
3. What is the SWOT analysis of this market?
4. What are the major characteristics of the market?
5. How these characteristics are adding value to our company?
6. How these characteristic of the market would support us in improving our revenues and profitability?
7. How operations in this market would reduce the costs of business?
8. What is the sustainability of these characteristics?
9. What is the sensitivity of these market characteristics?
10. How has this market behaved in past for similar offerings like ours? What are our expectations about its behavior now?
11. How future events could affect these characteristics?
12. How these events would affect us?
13. What is the average range of earnings in these markets?
14. How these geographical markets would affect our ability for expansion and innovation?
15. What are our fixed and variable costs in these markets?

16. How these costs would affect our profitability?

Our Offering's Uniqueness

Specify the uniqueness of our products and services. Specify the main features which would contribute to the strength of these offerings in the market.

Points for Discussion

1. What is the difference between our company's and competitor's offerings?
2. How our products and services are better than competitors?
3. If our competitor's offerings are better than us, what should we do to bridge this gap?
4. What is the demand of Customer Segment?
5. What makes us sure about these demands of customers?
6. What is the understanding of other players of industry about customer demand?
7. How is our offering different from available options?
8. Why our product would fill the gap in the market?
9. Why our product would get success in market?
10. If our product is successful then how soon would competitors catch us?
11. How can we monetize our offerings in the lead time available to us?
12. What marketing and sales effort would be required for this monetization?
13. What is our plan?
14. How would we able to maintain the differentiation?
15. How new features and services can help us in creating differentiation?

Target Market's Purchasing Power

Specify the purchasing capacity of our target market. Specify the facts which prove the strength of target customer segment to keep our business profitable and growing.

Points for Discussion

1. What is the market size of potential buyers?
2. Will they buy our offering at the present level of pricing?
3. Which research and analysis proves this point?
4. What is the total expenditure of this customer segment in our product line?
5. What are the possible ways to increase this expenditure level?
6. What is our breakeven point of the product or service?
7. What is the total earning potential of this offering during its lifetime?
8. What is the product life cycle of the product?
9. What factors would affect the purchasing power of the customer segment?
10. Is this customer segment a risk or an opportunity?
11. How can we mitigate the risks?
12. How can our risks be managed over the whole product range of our company?

Sales Estimates

Specify the sales projections of our company for next five years. Describe the reasons for our optimism to meet these projections.

Points for Discussion

1. What is our prediction of market behavior over next 1, 3 and 5 years?
2. What major changes can be expected during this time period? How our offering would evolve during this time period?
3. How the market would evolve?
4. How the consumer need and demand would change?
5. What is our sales forecast for next five years?
6. How would the cost behave during this time?
7. What can we do to improve our profitability during this time?
8. What are our assumptions?
9. What are the reasons for these assumptions?
10. What are the main assumptions of industry players?
11. How are they different from our assumptions?
12. What is the sensitivity of our assumptions?
13. How would our sales estimates would be affected by demographics, economy, government rules and regulation?
14. How do we forecast?
15. What are our arguments about using the present method of forecasting?
16. How other forecasting methods would change our sales estimates?
17. Are our earnings estimates conservative and costs inflated?

Evidence for Sales Estimates

Produce the evidence with supporting documents for the genuineness of our sales forecast.

Points for Discussion

1. Do we have any comparable real case in industry which can prove our sales estimates?
2. Do we have the track record to perform and achieve our sales estimates as planned?
3. What skills and competencies would be required for achieving our sales estimates?
4. How would we able to get those skills and competencies?
5. Would we have enough resources to get these skills?
6. Why other companies were not able to achieve these sales estimates? What right are we doing to achieve it?
7. What is our learning from other markets?

OPERATIONS

Product Line

Describe the product and service our company provides. Specify the needs and demands of market which our product line satisfies.

Points for Discussion

1. What is the description of our offerings?

2. Where our offerings are placed in the product profile of the industry?
3. How do these offerings fare in the industry?
4. What is the R&D investment of this product line?
5. How are the products and services developed in the industry?
6. What is the process of improvisation of these offerings?
7. What resources are required for improvisation of these offerings? Do we have those resources?
8. If not, how will we arrange for those resources?
9. What operational skills and competencies would be required? Do we have these skills and competencies?
10. If not, how can we arrange for these skills and competencies?
11. How would we arrange for the required funds?
12. How our production of other products would support our development of new products and services?
13. Which operational processes would be required for the development of the product?
14. What percentage of the product can be customized?
15. What percentage of the product can be personalized?
16. How much flexibility do we have to customize the products for customers?
17. What percentage of products is returned by customers due to various reasons?
18. What are the main reasons for returning the products by customers?
19. What is our learning from the returned products?
20. How can we reduce the percentage of returned products?
21. How do we manage the process of returned products?

22. What do we do with the returned products? Can we rework on them to sell again?
23. How can we improve our operations to meet the changing requirements of the market?
24. How are the operations of industry players better or worse than us?
25. How are they operationally different from us?
26. How fast can we meet the updated requirements of the market? How is it compared to industry?
27. How this ability would help us in capturing market share for our offerings?

Competitive Advantage

Specify the advantages of the company's location. Describe the reasons for choosing the present location and plans to utilize it to gain competitive advantage in the market.

Points for Discussion

1. What are the locations of corporate office, operations and sales?
2. Why the specific location of operations is chosen?
3. How many manufacturing locations do we have? What are the reasons for the numbers of manufacturing locations?
4. How many sales offices do we have? How these locations are optimally used to drive maximum business?
5. What are the pros and cons of these locations of sales and operations?
6. What are the locations of main operations of competitors?
7. What are the advantages and disadvantage of these locations?
8. What is the cost benefit analysis of all these locations?
9. Which player in the industry, including us, has the best location of operations and sales?
10. How does our location of manufacturing units would affect my sourcing?
11. Where do we store our raw materials and finished good?
12. How our equipment and machinery is maintained?
13. How does the location of operations affect my manufacturing?
14. How the location of operations affects my delivery of goods?

15. How this location would help us in serving our customers better?
16. What limitations this location offers?
17. How can I take advantage of the positive factors? How best can I manage the negative factors?
18. Do we have better options for locating our operations and sales?
19. By what percentage our operations would improve with these options?

Production Process

Describe the production process of our company. Specify the major steps in production and its productivity in comparison to other industry players.

Points for Discussion

1. What is our production process?
2. How is it in comparison to other players in industries?
3. If production process is unproductive, then what are the reasons for that?
4. How can we improve our production process?
5. What can we learn about production process from other industries?
6. Why haven't we implemented these ideas till now?
7. What are the best processes and practices of production countrywide?
8. What are the best processes and practices of production internationally?
9. What is the wastage percentage in production and how is it in comparison with industry average?
10. If our wastage is higher than industry average then what are the reasons for the difference?
11. How technology is used in production process?
12. How is our usage of technology in comparison to industry?
13. How technology improves our productivity?
14. Which mathematical models are we using to manage productivity?
15. How these models help us to measure and manage our production?
16. How flexible is our production, can it be adjusted based upon market demand?
17. What do we need to do to make our production flexible?

18. How will our production costs be affected with flexibility?
19. How can we manage the quality of products with flexibility?
20. How can we measure and manage the costs of product during production?
21. How can we measure and manage the quality of product during production?
22. Which management tools and methods do we use?
23. Are these management tools and methods working for us?
24. How these methods would help us in managing the quality?
25. How can management methods help us in managing our costs?
26. How can we implement kaizen in production?
27. How will we able to manage and implement small improvements in production?
28. How do we keep workers motivated on shop floor?
29. Do we meet required manufacturing standards?
30. If not, what do we need to do to get our manufacturing certified by required authorities?
31. How these certifications would help us in business by increasing sales?
32. How more automation would help us with productivity?
33. What level of automation can we implement in our production?
34. How this automation would improve our productivity?
35. Can we move a part of our manufacturing offshore?
36. Which processes can be moved offshore?
37. How can we do that?
38. How can we manage it to get maximum advantage?
39. What cost advantage would be we get with offshoring?
40. How would our business systems change with offshoring?
41. How government regulations would affect us with offshoring?

42. What is our manpower requirement for production?
43. What skills and competencies do we require for production?
44. Are we able to get skilled manpower at our manufacturing location?
45. How can we manage the shortage of skilled manpower in production?
46. How our competitors managing it?
47. How our competitors get the advantage of location?
48. How do we manage raw materials procurement?
49. How are our raw material sourced?
50. How our vendors are selected?
51. What is our vendor management process?
52. What is the bargaining power of vendors?
53. Do we have single or multiple vendors?
54. What are our reasons for that?
55. What are the pros and cons for selecting single or multiple vendors?
56. What are the risks?
57. How can we manage these risks?
58. What are the best practices of industry to manage vendors?
59. How many competitors use common vendors?
60. How does it affect us?
61. What is the cost of raw material? Is it higher than other big players?
62. How would this higher cost affect us?
63. How can we manage the higher cost of raw material?
64. How are our relations with vendors?
65. How are they paid? What is the credit period?
66. Do vendors complain about the credit period?
67. What are our plans to manage them better?
68. What control do we have in vendor's business?
69. How much control do big players of the industry have in vendor's business?
70. How the control of big players in vendor's business would affect us?

71. What type of service agreement do we have with them?
72. How are these agreements in comparison to competitors?
73. What do we need to do to improve our service agreement with vendors?
74. How can we beat competitors with better service agreements with vendors?
75. Are these vendors ready to support us by changing their business processes to synchronize with our production processes?
76. Can we import a part of our raw material?
77. How would it impact our costs and processes?
78. How do we manage our inventory?
79. What is our inventory management cost?
80. How is it in comparison with other players?
81. Are we using the best practices of inventory management?
82. What is wastage in inventory?
83. Is our inventory management different for raw materials and finished goods?
84. How fast our inventory moves?
85. Are there any cases of theft?
86. How can we reduce these cases of theft?
87. What steps have we taken?
88. What is our point of sale and point of distribution?
89. How our products are distributed?
90. Which channels are used for distribution?
91. What channels are used by competitors?
92. Which distribution channels are considered as best?
93. Are we using the best practices of distribution?
94. Are our distribution processes efficient? What can we do to improve efficiency?
95. What technology are we using?
96. How technology improves productivity of distribution?
97. How can we utilize the latest technologies to improve our distribution productivity?

98. Can we decrease the levels in distribution channel? How would it impact our costs and quality?
99. Can we develop new and better distribution channels?
100. What are those?
101. How can we implement these new distribution channels?
102. What would be the initial cost to develop these channels?
103. What would be the total cost saving over a period of time?
104. What is the cost-benefit-analysis of these new distribution channels?
105. What are the risks?
106. How can we mitigate these risks?
107. What is the satisfaction level of customers?
108. What are the complaints of customers?
109. What actions have we taken to resolve these complaints?
110. How can we make sure that these complaints are not repeated?
111. What problems are faced by industry in distribution?
112. What actions are taken by industry players to resolve these problems?

SUPPORT

Keys to success in Production

Describe the key success factors for success of production in our industry and specify the reasons for the high productivity of our production process.

Points for Discussion

1. How many processes do we have in production?
2. How efficient and effective are these processes?
3. How are these in comparison to best processes in industry and compared to other industries?
4. What should we do to implement best production processes in our company?
5. What are the key result areas (KRAs) and the key success factors (KSFs) of these processes?
6. What are our KRAs and KSFs?
7. What is employee productivity of industry?
8. What is our employee productivity? How it is in comparison to industry?
9. What is the employee productivity of best players of industry?
10. What we need to do to improve it?
11. What efforts we have taken till now to improve it?
12. What is our improvement percentage in employee productivity?
13. Where do we stand in comparison to industry in quality of equipment and machinery?
14. What we need to do to improve it?

Competitive Advantage of Production Process

Specify the uniqueness of our production process and describe the competitive advantage it provides to us.

Points for Discussion

1. How can the production process be the competitive advantage in our industry?
2. How is this unique?
3. How could that production process be made more efficient?
4. How can the costs of this process be reduced?
5. What are the productivity levels of production processes in industry?
6. What is our productivity of production process?
7. What is the productivity of our competitors?
8. What can we learn from our competitor's processes of production?
9. How can we create an edge in market with production productivity?
10. What unique are we doing to get that edge?
11. How can we maintain that edge?
12. What resources would be required to improve this edge?
13. Will these resources be internal or external?
14. How can we increase the component of internal resources? (To maintain the trade secrets)
15. How do we do the cost-benefit-analysis of improvements in production process?
16. How can this competitive advantage in production help us in maintaining our strength in other areas of business?
17. What can we do to maintain this competitive advantage?

18. How competitive advantage affects the moral of employees?
19. How production competitive advantage improves productivity?
20. How is gross profit margin or contribution margin in comparison to other players on major products?
21. How can we make it better?
22. If some player in industry has better margins than us then what are the reasons for their better performance?
23. What can we learn from these companies?
24. What are these ratios for other products?
25. If we have better lead then what can we do to maintain this lead?

Services

Specify the steps required for providing the service. Specify our uniqueness in operating procedures of services which act as a competitive advantage for us.

Points for Discussion

1. What services do we offer to market?
2. What is required to offer these services?
3. What demand and need it satisfies in the market?
4. What are the various stages to provide the service?
5. What steps are involved at each stage of providing the service?
6. What are the key success factors for our service?
7. How can we make our services as our competitive advantage?
8. What is the performance of our services?
9. How our services are rated by customers?
10. Do we outsource a part of our services?
11. How do we calculate the costs of providing the services?
12. What skills are required to provide the services?
13. How do we source this skill set?
14. What is our personnel cost to provide the service?
15. What assurances do we give to our consumers about services?
16. What are our fixed and variable costs?
17. What are the ratios for fixed and variable costs?
18. What is the optimum ratio for fixed and variable costs?
19. How can we improve our cost ratio?
20. What are our profit margins?
21. How can we maintain these margins?
22. What is the breakeven level of the service revenue of the company

23. How do we measure and maintain our costs for providing the services?

Merchandising Category

Specify the merchandising category of our business and describe its major offerings.

Points for Discussion

1. What is the merchandizing category?
2. What are the major offerings and product line?
3. Which niche or customer segment it serves?
4. Where are we placed in the market share of the product?
5. How the market forces affect this product line and our business?
6. How can we identify the risks in this line?
7. How can we mitigate these risks?
8. What type of networking is required in this industry?
9. Do we have the required networking?
10. What is required to get the networking?

Competitive Advantage of Products

Describe the product and product line and other offerings of our company. Specify the competitive advantage which this product line provides to us. Mention our strategy to maintain this competitive advantage in our industry.

Points for Discussion

1. What are the unique features of this product line?
2. How this product line would help us in getting more revenues and profits?
3. Does this product line offer any competitive advantage for us?
4. How can this competitive advantage be maintained?
5. What we need to do about it?
6. Which factors can stamp out this competitive advantage?
7. What can we do to protect this advantage?

Selling Strategy

Specify the selling strategy of our company. Describe our expectations from this strategy and reasons for its robustness.

Points for Discussion

1. How products and services are sold in our industry?
2. Do competitors sell differently?
3. What are the reasons for this difference in selling techniques by competitors?
4. How these techniques benefit our competitors?
5. What can we learn from these techniques?
6. How do we sell?
7. Are we better than our competitors in selling or worse? Why?
8. What is the cost-benefit-analysis of these selling techniques?
9. What is the impact of these techniques?
10. How does it help to build better connections with customers?
11. Is our sale push, pull or the combination of both?
12. How our experiences and learning of the previous years has improved our selling?
13. What were our main insights from this experience?
14. What do we need to do to keep learning from our experiences in sales?
15. What initiatives we have taken from these experiences?
16. What are the results of these initiatives?
17. How have we developed our selling strategy?
18. Who were the people involved in development of selling strategy?
19. Did we capture all required information and insights to develop it?

20. What is our methodology to develop it?
21. Which methodology is used by other industry players?
22. Are the methodologies of other industry players working for them?
23. How is our methodology in comparison to other industry players?
24. How can we make sure to improve our strategy and execution?
25. How good is our sales team?
26. How is this team trained?
27. How we capture the learning and experiences of sales team?
28. How the learning of sales team about market is transferred to marketing?
29. How is our sales team monitored?
30. What is the attrition rate of the sales team?
31. What are the main reasons of this attrition rate?
32. How is attrition rate of sales team compared to industry?
33. What are the reasons of this difference in attrition rate?
34. How can we reduce the attrition rate of our sales team?
35. What are the touch points of sales team with customers?
36. How can we utilize these touch points?
37. What mistakes we do at these touch points?
38. What we need to do to be faultless at touch points?
39. What can we learn for other players to extract the maximum value from these touch points?
40. What can learn from other industries about these touch points?
41. How technology and new management techniques can help us to improve our productivity at these touch points?

42. What we need to do to implement these techniques and technologies?
43. What would be our expected improve in productivity?

Company's Physical Facilities

Specify the reasons for the company's physical facilities and their contribution in improving the efficiency of company's operations.

Points for Discussion

1. What is the layout of our company's operations?
2. How was this layout designed?
3. What are the reasons for this design?
4. How is this design in comparison to others?
5. How is this design adding value to our company?
6. Have we used the best practices and best design presently available?
7. If not, what are the reasons?
8. What can we do about it?

Purchasing

Describe the purchasing methodology of the company and specify the reasons for its effectiveness.

Points for Discussion

1. What material is purchased by the company?
2. Which material has the maximum value?
3. What effect purchasing has on our company?
4. Which purchasing procedures and processes our company uses?
5. How are these purchasing procedures and processes in comparison to other companies?
6. What can we learn from others processes and procedures of purchasing?
7. What are the purchasing best practices of other sectors and industries?
8. What can we learn from best practices of other sectors and industries?
9. How can they be tested and implemented?
10. How can we make these practices and processes of purchasing more efficient and cost effective?
11. What would be our cost advantage, in comparison to industry, if we implement them?
12. How these procedures affect our relation with our vendors?
13. How has the behavior of vendors changed for us?
14. What we need to do to improve it?
15. How technology usage would improve us in purchasing while reducing costs?
16. How well is purchasing integrated with our operations and sales?
17. What problems we face with integration of purchasing with other departments?
18. What we need to do to improve this integration?

19. How do we ensure the quality of purchased material?
20. What is our procedure to return the low quality purchased material?
21. What is our credit period which is negotiated with our vendors?
22. What was the objective of these negotiations and how does it help us in business?
23. What net benefits we have got from these negotiations with vendors?
24. Are we getting the best prices of the purchased material?
25. If no, then what are the reasons for that?
26. What we need to do to get the best prices of purchased material?

Inventory Management

Describe the inventory management system of our company. Mention the reasons for its effectiveness in cost reduction for our company.

Quality Control

Specify the quality control systems of our company and the reasons for their effectiveness in maintaining the quality of company's products and services.

Customer Service

Specify the customer service systems of our company and the reasons for their effectiveness in ensuring the satisfaction of customers.

Personnel

Specify the personnel details of the company, which includes management and other employees.

Points for Discussion

1. What are the top level management positions in the company?
2. What are the primary duties and responsibilities of top level managers and officials?
3. Who holds top managerial positions?
4. What are the job qualifications required for each position?
5. What is the track record of each manager?
6. What unique contribution does each position holder make to the success of the company?
7. What is the salary of each manager and executive?
8. What is the salary breakup?
9. What is our future personnel plan?
10. What is the reason for this personnel plan?

Financing Profile

Specify the financing and its type required by the company. Describe the reason for it. Also, specify the achievements of the company.

<u>Points for Discussion</u>

1. Specify a brief review of the company's past financial performance, as measured by the growth in cash flow and profit, and current financial position.
2. Specify the financial goals for the company's planning period.
3. Define the external financing required to support planned operations of the company.
4. Specify the working capital requirement for the planned period.
5. Define the type, category and maturity of the required financing. Specify the proportion of each type of financing.
6. Specify the expected sources of this financing; the existing proportions of the debt and owner's equity capital used to finance the company.
7. Specify the projected proportion of the debt and equity capital after the proposed financing.
8. Specify the projected cash flow and profit levels or growth rates.
9. Describe any considerations or planned actions that have major financial consequences such as liability of a pending lawsuit, a change in financial strategy, or the intention to take the company to public?
10. What has been company's financial performance for the past three years as measured by the trend in the key ration values such as the growth rate of cash flow and profit, or ROI?

11. What is the current financial position as measured by the key indicators such as cash flow from operations, profit margin and debt ratio?

OPERATING PLANS

INDUSTRY ANALYSIS

New Entrants

Describe the potential of industry by discussing the new entrants in the industry. Specify the reasons and projections of these new entrants.

Points for Discussion

1. How many companies entered the industry in past three years?
2. What are their main offerings?
3. What are their main reasons for entry? What is their main market?
4. What potential they see in the market?
5. What potential can we estimate about industry from our observation of these new entrants?
6. What is our reason of entry?
7. Is it same as these new entrants or different than those?
8. If different, then what are the reasons for this difference?
9. How are these companies performing?
10. If they are successful, what right they did; if unsuccessful, then what wrong they did?
11. What is our learning from the observation of these new companies?
12. What is total money gained or lost by these companies?
13. How their valuation has changes over the years?
14. How many companies are entering the industry with us?
15. What are their main reasons of entry? Where do they see the potential?

16. What is their strategy and plans?
17. How would we rate them on resources? Are these stronger or weaker than us?
18. How their entry would affect us?
19. How many companies are expected to enter the industry in coming years?
20. What are the reasons for that?
21. How would it affect out plans?

New offerings and innovations

Specify the new products and services which are launched in the market in recent time. Define the reasons for these new launches and their acceptance in the market.

Points for Discussion

1. Is our industry innovative?
2. How can we say that?
3. Which trends affect the industry's innovations?
4. Which trends are visible in industry now?
5. How demand in the industry changes with trends?
6. How offerings in the industry changes with trends?
7. How fast the industry meets the new demand of the market?
8. How the offerings are evolving?
9. Which are the latest offerings from the industry?
10. How the latest trends have affected these offerings?
11. What is the profitability of these products?
12. Did other new and established companies enter the market to serve the new demand of the market?
13. What is the success ratio of these companies?
14. How are we different from these companies?
15. How this difference increases our probability of success?
16. How innovative is this industry in comparison to other industries and sectors?
17. What factors lead to the innovation in offerings?
18. What are the processes which companies use to create innovative offerings?
19. What is our process to develop innovative offerings?

20. What is the ROI (Return on Investment) on innovation investment for industry and major players?
21. What is the ROI on innovation investment for us?
22. How customers react to innovations in the market?
23. Are these innovations are incremental improvements or new offerings?

Technological Obsolescence

Specify the time of technological obsolescence for the industry. Describe the reasons for it and plans of industry players to deal with it.

Points for Discussion

1. How much technology is involved in offering?
2. How this technology is evolving?
3. How technology has evolved in the past?
4. How usage of technology changed the competitive factors in the industry?
5. How companies of the industry use technology in innovative ways to be more competitive?
6. How the evolution of technology in our industry is forecasted for the future?
7. How this technology is related to other industries like IT?
8. What is the average time of technology obsolescence in our industry?
9. What is the present status of technology in our industry?
10. What can we learn from this phase?
11. What is the ROI of technology usage for our company? Is it expected and positive?
12. If ROI is not as per expectations then what needs to be done?
13. How would we manage the entry of any disruptive technology?
14. What we need to do to prepare ourselves for that?
15. What resources would be required for that?
16. How these resources would be arranged?
17. How other companies have prepared themselves for any disruptive technology?
18. How are we using the latest technology?

19. Are we consistently improvising and working with latest technologies to capture the market with fresh ideas and new technologies?
20. How would we calculate the value and robustness of new technologies?
21. How would we integrate our offerings with new technology?
22. What is our strategy to take advantage of any changes in technology?
23. Can we have competitive advantage of regeneration of offerings with any new stable technology?
24. What we need to do to equip ourselves with this competitive advantage?

Technological Changes

Specify the technological changes in industry in recent time. Describe its impact on industry players and their strategies to utilize these changes.

Points for Discussion

1. How the technology has changed in past three years in our industry?
2. What are the reasons for these changes in technology?
3. Which are the key factors which lead these changes in technology in industry?
4. Who could take the advantages of these changes in technologies and evolved as winners?
5. What was the uniqueness of planning and execution of these winners? How could they have this uniqueness?
6. What are the reasons of these technological changes?
7. What is our learning from these changes?
8. Are these technological changes are influenced by other industries or self-created?
9. What are the leading indicators which can indicate us any changes to come?
10. Is this technology changes due to government intervention or private investments?
11. How this technology affects other industries?
12. Over the years, how Research & Development investment has changed in this technology? What are the reasons for that?
13. How R&D investment has affected the speed of technology development?
14. What are the major changes in technology, incremental or disruptive?

Supply Chain

Describe the supply chain of the industry. Mention the reasons for its effectiveness and its influence in success of our company.

Points for Discussion

1. What is the supply chain of the industry?
2. How can the value chain of the industry be defined?
3. What are the components of supply chain?
4. What is the supply chain for our offerings?
5. Who are the players of supply chain? What value they add to offerings?
6. Is our supply chain efficient? How would we rate the efficiency of supply chain in comparison to other supply chains of industry? How is this in comparison to other industries?
7. How does supply chain influences our cost?
8. How does it affect our pricing?
9. What can we do to reduce our supply chain costs?

Suppliers

Specify the names of major suppliers of the industry. Describe their influence and bargaining power and its impact on us. Mention your risk management plan to manage the complexities of supply chain.

Points for Discussion

1. What material is required for our offerings?
2. Who are the main suppliers for that material?
3. In which sector would they be categorized?
4. What are the main components to be supplied?
5. What is the importance of each supplier for our offerings?
6. Do we have multiple suppliers to reduce our risk?
7. If not, what do we need to do to have multiple suppliers?
8. How is our relation to our suppliers? How does this affect us? What can we do to enhance it?
9. What is the risk associated with these suppliers?
10. What is our plan to manage these risks?
11. Who are the main suppliers in industry?
12. Are these major suppliers reliable?
13. What can affect their reliability?
14. What is their influence in our industry?
15. Do they supply us? If not, what are the reasons?
16. How does that affect us?
17. How the supply side has changed over the years for our industry?
18. How would it change and evolve with time?
19. How does it affect us and what do we need to do to take the maximum benefits?

Distribution Channel

Specify the main distribution channels of the industry. Describe the ways our company uses these channels to satisfy customers.

Points for Discussion

1. How products are distributed in the industry?
2. What are the channels through which the products are distributed?
3. How much is distributed from each channel?
4. Which distribution channels are managed by the company?
5. Which distribution channels are outsourced?
6. Which of these channels are best in performance?
7. Which of these channels are worst in performance?
8. What are the reasons of best and worst performance of these channels?
9. How worst performing channels can be improved?
10. How can we assure the best possible distribution of our offerings?
11. How fast our products are distributed?
12. What is the customer's feedback about the distribution experience?
13. What are the main reasons for this feedback?
14. How we have used this feedback to improve ourselves?
15. Is our distribution channel robust enough? Have we tested it with worst case scenarios?
16. How similar products are distributed in other industries? What can we learn from that?
17. What is the cost involved in distribution?
18. Can we reduce the cost of distribution without reducing the efficiency of distribution?

19. How can these channels be used to receive feedback from customers?
20. Can we use these channels in any way to serve our customers better?

Scope of Market

Describe the scope of market for industry's products and services.

Points for Discussion

1. How big is the projected market for our products and services?
2. What is the size of the market in our current geographical reach?
3. What is our market share in market?
4. What are the reasons for this market share?
5. Who is the market leader for our industry?
6. What is the maximum profitability which we can get from this product line?
7. What we need to do get this maximum profitability?
8. Are we missing any opportunity to increase our sales in the market?
9. What factors can weaken or strengthen this opportunity?
10. How can we capture a part of our competitor's market share?
11. What reasons can contribute to that?
12. How would competitors react to that?
13. How can we manage these risks?

Primary Customers

Describe the characteristics of the customers of the industry. Specify our strategy to attract their attention toward our offerings.

Points for Discussion

1. Define the Target Customer Segment (TCS)?
2. Who are the main customers?
3. How do these customers rate us in industry?
4. What do TCS feel about our offerings?
5. What could be the strategy of competitors to attract our customers?
6. How can respond to their strategies?
7. In what way our offerings satisfy our customers?
8. What are the buying characteristics of these customers?
9. What customer data are we capturing and analyzing?
10. What information are we able to generate from this information?
11. How similar data is used for analysis worldwide?
12. Can we use this data to generate more insights?
13. How can we use this information and insights to take decisions?
14. How would it help to take better decisions?
15. How can we use this information to increase the sales of our products?

Influence on Customers

Specify the main factors which influence the purchasing behavior of customers. Describe our plan to utilize this behavior to increase our sales.

Points for Discussion

1. How can we define the buyer of our offerings?
2. Who is the consumer of our offering? How our offering is consumed?
3. Who is the influencer in the buying decisions?
4. What are the characteristics of heavy buyers of our offering? Why do they buy this amount?
5. What are the characteristics of customers who consume less? How can their consumption be increased?
6. Why some past customers have stopped buying our products?
7. What products, services or substitutes are these customers using to satisfy their needs?
8. What factors lead to increase in buying by customers?
9. What factors lead to decrease in buying by customers?
10. What add-ons in products or services would increase the sale of our offerings?
11. What is the cost-benefit-analysis for these add-ons?
12. In past, what factors led to rejection of any product or service by TCS?
13. How does negative propaganda against our offering or industry affects TCS?
14. Who could be the sponsor of negative propaganda against us or industry?
15. What would be our plan to face it, if such propaganda is directed against us?

16. Are we equipped to take such action?
17. What are the risks for such action?
18. How can these risks be mitigated?
19. How different seasons and festivals affect the sale of our offerings?
20. How TCS respond to promotions?
21. Which types of promotions are most effective?
22. How active are we in promotional activities? What is our promotional plan for next one year?
23. How pricing affects our sales?
24. How does competitors use pricing for improving profitability and increasing market share?
25. What is our pricing in comparison to competitors?
26. How our offerings are better priced?
27. Do we have competition from low cost players?
28. How customers respond to low cost players?
29. What is our strategy to face them?
30. How does import from other countries affects our sales and pricing?
31. What is our strategy to compete with imported products?
32. How brand image affects the sales and margins on our products?
33. Are TCS brand conscious? By what percentage are they ready to pay for premium brand?
34. How do we rate our brand equity in industry?
35. How media opinion affects sales?
36. What steps we need to take to keep it favorable?

Factors Influencing the Industry

Specify the major demographic, economic and competitive factors which influence our industry. Describe our strategy to utilize these factors for our success.

Points for Discussion

1. How economic cycles affect our industry?
2. How economic factors affect the sale of our products and services?
3. Which economic indicators impact us maximum?
4. How can we prepare ourselves for economic weaknesses?
5. Historically, what is the average recovery time for economy?
6. What is our business continuity plan?
7. What are the competitive forces which affects the industry and our offerings?
8. How these competitive forces behave?
9. How best can we manage ourselves among these forces?
10. Can we take advantage of these forces to improve our sales?
11. What demographic factors affect industry and sales?
12. Which are the main demographic factors? How do they behave?
13. What are the main reasons for their changes? How fast do they change?
14. How these changes in main demographic factors affect us?
15. Which market and social forces affect the demographic factors?
16. How can we use these insights to forecast better?

17. How our market and industry are linked to national and international economy?
18. How strength and weakness of international events affect us?

Trends of Factors Influencing the Industry

Specify the trends which influence the industry. Describe our system which is able to exploit these trends to modify our offerings to suit market requirement.

Points for Discussion

1. What are the major trends which affects industry and our sales?
2. How these trends change?
3. How fast these trends change?
4. What are the reasons for these trends to change?
5. Which trends can we identify now?
6. What these trends indicate for our industry?
7. How other players of industry are reacting to it? What are the main reasons for that?
8. How can we use the insight from trends for improving our business?
9. What is our prediction about these trends for next two years?
10. Are we checking these trends with different scenarios?
11. How can we prepare ourselves to take the benefit of these trends?
12. How other players are interpreting these trends?
13. What actions are these players taking to utilize these trends for their benefit?
14. How our customers react to trends?
15. How fast these trends affect their buying habits?
16. Who are the lead people (among customers) to accept these trends?
17. How would we interpret the behavior of these lead people?

Present Behavior of the Factors Influencing the Industry

Specify the facts which prove any changes in the key industry factors. Mention our plan to utilize these changes to capture the market.

Points for Discussion

1. What are the key industry factors?
2. How the behaviors of these industry factors affect us?
3. How are these factors calculated?
4. How is the data from these factors analyzed?
5. What factors are we able to observe now in market?
6. What do these factors indicate?
7. How can these factors be interpreted for industry and us?
8. How do we need to act on these factors?
9. What is the history of these factors and what do they indicate now?
10. What prediction do we have about them for the future?
11. How other players are looking at these factors?
12. How do they plan to act on these factors?
13. How can we observe the changes in these factors and what can we do about it?

Past Performance of Industry

Specify the past performance of industry. Mention the main financial parameters to prove the performance trends.

Points for Discussion

1. What is the performance of industry in the last few years?
2. What is the trend of cost, revenue and profit for industry?
3. How these trends are related to other industries and macroeconomic indicators?
4. What are the interpretations of these trends?
5. What the reasons for these trends?
6. How our sales and product-line have fared during last few years? What are the reasons for the observed trends? What method we use to calculate it?
7. How can we use this analysis in business forecasting?
8. What are the main reasons for the cost behavior?
9. What are the main reasons for the observed behavior of revenues?
10. How others players are affected by this behavior? Why?
11. How these insights would help us creating better strategy?

Industry Forecast

Mention the forecast of industry calculated from primary and secondary research. Describe the sync of our strategy with this forecast of industry.

Points for Discussion

1. What is our forecast for industry and offerings?
2. What methodology we use to calculate this forecast?
3. What is the forecast of other players and experts about industry?
4. How is their forecast different from ours?
5. What are the reasons for this difference in forecast?
6. How has this forecast impacted the strategy and plans of others?
7. How our strategy and plans would change due to these forecasts?
8. If this forecast proves to be incorrect, how would that affect us?
9. What are the main factors which can affect our forecasting?
10. Which are our main assumptions?
11. What is the probability level of each assumption?
12. Which are the main assumptions in calculations of forecasting?
13. What we need to do to continuously updating our forecasting based upon assumptions?
14. How can we use the best practices of other industries and markets for improving our forecasting methodology?

Assumptions of Forecast

Specify the assumptions for industry forecast. Describe the logic for these assumptions and the reasons for our confidence.

Points for Discussion

1. What are the major reasons for these forecasts?
2. How can we say that these forecasts are achievable?
3. What are the assumptions of our competitors?
4. How are we different from our competitors in forecasting?
5. What are the reasons for these differences?
6. What can we learn from our competitors and others to improve our outlook?
7. Have we analyzed in depth by using various scenarios and assumptions?
8. Which are the best and worst scenarios?
9. Are we prepared and equipped for the worst scenario?
10. What do we need to do to achieve these forecasts?

Strategic Opportunity in Industry

Specify the opportunities in the industry which can be used by the industry players by offering various products and services.

Points for Discussion

1. What are the opportunities in our industry which are yet to be tapped?
2. What is gap or unsatisfied need in the market which pointing to opportunity?
3. Why is this opportunity not tapped till now by any industry player?
4. How are these industry players looking at this potential opportunity?
5. What are the reasons which are resisting them to fill this gap in the market?
6. Is it that we are missing something in analyzing the need of the market?
7. Which are the new companies which are trying to enter the market for this opportunity?
8. What is the basic reason of these new companies to enter the market? What are their plans to get success?
9. What are the expectations of these companies from the market? When would they achieve breakeven and when would they be profitable?
10. Can we compare the similar scenario with any other industry, for better learning?
11. What can we learn from the experience of industry with previous opportunities?
12. What was the potential of each opportunity and how it affected the dynamics of the industry?
13. What is our learning from these past opportunities of the industry?

14. How much money is chasing these opportunities?
15. How investors are reacting to these opportunities? What is the number of serious investors?
16. What is the plan of investors to multiply their money using these opportunities?
17. How other financial sectors like venture capitalists, private equity funds and banks are looking at these opportunities? What are their reasons?
18. What are their investment plans? What are their exit plans?
19. Is there something which is missed by everyone and we can use?
20. How valuations of the companies from our industry would rise in the future?

Strategic Opportunity for Us

Specify the reasons for our success with these opportunities existing in industry. Describe our strategy to monetize these opportunities.

Points for Discussion

1. Why are we confident about our strategy?
2. Is our strategy robust?
3. Have we tested this strategy properly?
4. Is our strategy agile to meet any changes in market?
5. What are other player's strategies?
6. How are others strategies in comparison to us?
7. What do we need to do to beat our competitors in the marketplace?
8. What are major threats to the industry?
9. What strategies do the major companies in the industry use to protect against these threats?
10. What strategies would the company use to protect against these threats?
11. What is the SWOT (Strengths, Weaknesses, Opportunities and Threats) of our company?
12. How our strategy tackles our weaknesses and threats?
13. How our strategy strengthens our strengths and makes us dynamic enough to exploit the opportunities in the market place?

MARKET ANALYSIS AND SALES FORECAST

Market

Describe our market. Specify the reasons for our confidence of success in this market.

Points for Discussion

1. Define the market of the industry and our offerings to the market?
2. What is the total population of the market and what is the size of our market?
3. How our target customer segment (TCS) is geographical located? Are they concentrated at one place or spread out?
4. What is the earning potential of the market?
5. What we need to be to reach that potential of the market?
6. What can we do practically to reach near this potential in shortest possible time?
7. What is our expectation about this market? Will it increase or decrease?
8. What would be the factors responsible for increasing or decreasing the size of the market?
9. Which are the major factors?
10. What is the status of these factors now?
11. What are our expectations about these factors in the future?
12. How would those factors affect us in future?
13. Are we prepared and equipped to face it?
14. What reasons would be responsible for the increase or decrease in expenditure of customers, which could affect the sale of our products?
15. What issues would affect it?
16. How can we equip ourselves to face these challenges?

17. What is the size of the market which we are able to capture?
18. Can we work with industry associations to increase the size of the market?
19. Can we use some innovative tools and methods to increase the TCS expenditure on our products and services?

Market Demographics

Specify the demographic factors of the market.

Key Factors of Market

Specify the major factors like political, economic, social, legal and technical which would impact our business. Describe our plans to use these factors and trends for our growth.

Points for Discussion

1. What is the business landscape of the market?
2. What are the major forces affecting the business landscape?
3. What is the behavior of each force?
4. What factors affect each force?
5. What are the past trends of these factors?
6. What are they indicating now?
7. How are they affecting each force?
8. How these factors would affect our industry?
9. How these factors would affect us and other players of industry?
10. What can we do to either take advantage of these factors or protect ourselves?
11. How other players would deal with these factors?
12. Which are the key economic factors?
13. Which are the key social factors?
14. Which ones are the key legal factors affecting our industry?
15. How government view our industry in comparison to other industries?
16. What is the official government outlook about our industry?

17. What are the reasons for this outlook by government about our industry?
18. What rules, policies and regulations are placed by government on our industry?
19. What are the reasons for that?
20. What government is contemplating for the industry?
21. What bills related to industry are pending with government?
22. How strong are the lobbyists of our industry?
23. What are the demands of these lobbyists? What are the chances that their demands would be met?
24. How this would affect us? What are our plans to either use this for our growth or protect ourselves?
25. What are the major issues which could affect any of these factors?
26. What are the reasons and probability of happening for these issues?
27. Are there any events happening which could affect these factors?
28. What are the chances of these events to happen?
29. What can we do to be in better control than other?

Market Outlook

Describe the outlook of the market in terms of potential opportunities and financial parameters.

Points for Discussion

1. How target market is growing in revenues and profitability?
2. How target market is in comparison to other markets in industry and other industries?
3. What are the main reasons for the difference for this difference?
4. How has this market grown in the past?
5. What are the reasons for this growth?
6. What do we expect this market to grow in future?
7. What are the main reasons for this expectation?
8. What are the major factors driving this growth?
9. How are these factors looking now?
10. What media and other experts say about it?

Niche Market

Specify the market niche which our company targets. Describe your strategy for targeting this niche.

Points for Discussion

1. What are the demographic factors of the niche?
2. How advertisers target this niche? What are the reasons for it?
3. What channels they use and how they present their message?
4. What is the expected ROI of each of these channels of advertisements?
5. Which promotional strategies work on this niche?
6. To which promotional offers they react positively?
7. What is their view about our offerings?
8. How do they categorize our offering, a necessity, a regular or a luxury?
9. How can we develop a brand for this niche?
10. Which brands are top of their mind?
11. What is the strength of our brand for this niche?

Target Market Segment

Describe your target market, its demographic, psychographic, and behavioral characteristics. Specify our plans to connect with target market segment and to convince them to buy our products and services.

Points for Discussion

1. How can we communicate with our Target Customer Segment (TCS)?
2. What is the right channel to communicate with them?
3. What would be the right language and tone for communication with TCS?
4. What type of communication message they react to?
5. What would be the right way to communicate with them?
6. What is the negative communication for which we should be careful about?
7. Which communication has been most effective on them?
8. What were the reasons for the effectiveness of communication?
9. What idea we want to communicate to our target market?
10. What message should we use for communication?
11. How can we connect with them emotionally?
12. Where we want to position our offerings?

Our Strength in the Market

Specify our strength in the market. Specify the reasons for the success of our products and services in the market.

Points for Discussion

1. What is our USP (Unique Selling Proposition)?
2. Is this USP convincing?
3. How USP contribute in sales of our offerings?
4. Do Target Customer Segment (TCS) buy because of our USP?
5. What uniqueness we offer in our products and services?
6. Is this uniqueness appreciated by the TCS?
7. Are they ready to pay the right price for our offerings?
8. Why others cannot copy our USP?
9. What is our lead time for USP on which we can take advantage of selling?
10. Do we have something unique in our offerings which cannot be copied by competitors?
11. What is our competitive advantage?
12. What are the weaknesses of our competitor's offerings and how can we take advantage of that?
13. What TCS like and dislike about us and our competitors?
14. Is the market opportunity consistent with the company's general strategy?
15. Does the sales and profit potential of the market justifies the risks of the business?
16. What is our competitive advantage which justifies our entry into the market?
17. What abilities are required to successfully exploit the opportunity existing in the market? Does it have the necessary technical know-how, production

capacity, management and staff expertise, employee skills and financial resources?
18. What are the company's weaknesses which affect its chance for commercial success? If so, how can we overcome the weaknesses?
19. What pitfalls or risks are associated with this market opportunity? How these risks can be mitigated?

Revenues from Niche

Specify the revenues generated from this target segment. Describe the reasons for our optimism for the growth of sales volume from this segment.

Points for Discussion

1. How much this offering is contributing to our total revenues and profitability?
2. How can we improve it?
3. What are the reasons which are pulling it down?
4. What is the contribution of this specific niche to our revenues and profitability?
5. What is the potential of this niche?
6. How can we improve our earnings from this niche?
7. What we need to change or improve to enhance sales of our offering to niche?
8. Which products or services and which businesses represent the strongest competitive threat to the company?
9. On what basis (price, quality, service etc.) does the company's product or service compete?
10. What competitive advantage does the company hold over its competition?

Competitors

Describe the competition and its impact on our company. Describe our strategy to beat the competition.

Points for Discussion

1. Define our competition?
2. Which are our competitors?
3. Which are the major competitors?
4. What is the SWOT (Strengths, Weaknesses, Opportunities and Threats) of each of the competitor?
5. What are their strategies?
6. How their actions impact us?
7. What are the substitute products which are offered?
8. What is our competitive advantage over our competition?
9. What is our analysis about competitors based on following characteristics like:
    a. Location and appearance
    b. Selling price
    c. Financial strength
    d. The quality and type of customer service
    e. Customer relations
    f. Product or service differentiation
    g. Quality of employees
    h. Product or service quality
    i. Credit policy
    j. Reputation and image
    k. Advertising effectiveness

MARKETING PLAN

Company's Philosophy

Specify the purpose for company's existence. Specify its culture and values. Describe the reasons which would lead to our success following these values and culture.

Points for Discussion

1. What is the marketing philosophy of our company?
2. What is the marketing mission?
3. How marketing mission matches our corporate mission?
4. How do they support each other?
5. How this mission was created?
6. What was the process involved in creating this mission?
7. Who were the people involved in this creation?
8. How does it help us in taking marketing decisions and actions?
9. Do managers get into any contradiction while taking decisions? Why? What steps we need to take to solve it?
10. Is our marketing mission in any contradiction with external environment and forces?
11. If any contradiction exists then how would it affect us?
12. What actions do we need to take to rectify this mismatch?
13. What would be the cost (qualitative and quantitative) related to it?
14. How would it be communicated to all employees and stakeholders?
15. What is the process of this communication?
16. Is this is an effective process?
17. Can we find a better way to communicate?

Opportunity in Market

Describe the opportunities which exist in the market for the company's products, services and other offerings. Specify our plan to use these opportunities for our growth.

Points for Discussion

1. What demand exist in the market?
2. How strong is this demand?
3. Which segments of customers have this demand?
4. What products or services can satisfy this demand?
5. How much would they ready to pay for this demand?
6. Can this be considered as an opportunity?
7. Does it look like a profitable demand?
8. Is this opportunity visible to others?
9. How would they react to it?
10. How other companies are exploiting this opportunity?
11. Is this a short-term or long-term opportunity?
12. Can a business be built on this?
13. Will it help us to graduate to next level of growth?
14. What skills and competencies are required to exploit this opportunity?
15. Do we have required competencies to exploit this opportunities or we lack some?
16. How can we build these competencies in shortest possible time?
17. What trends are responsible for the creation of this demand in the market?
18. Do more of similar opportunities exist, which are not visible to us yet?
19. Do other opportunities exist in the market for our industry, maybe in other areas, which are not yet evident to us?

20. What can we do to identify these opportunities?
21. How can we use this insight to build market share and profitability?
22. How much time is required to develop these offerings, which include testing and beta launches?
23. How soon can we start work on this opportunity?
24. What will be the cost implications for this development and marketing? How would it affect our budget?
25. What events may cause this existing opportunity to go?
26. What is the probability of these events to occur?
27. How can we protect ourselves from the occurring of these events?
28. What steps do we need to take to protect ourselves from this loss?
29. What risks are associated with these opportunities?
30. How can we mitigate these risks?
31. How our offerings would satisfy the demand?
32. What are the ways to delight the customer segment?
33. What is the dollar value of opportunity?
34. How have we calculated this dollar value?
35. How much do we expect to earn from this opportunity?
36. What is the cost-benefit-analysis for this opportunity?
37. Do we need to make any changes in our offerings to serve our customers better?
38. Are we equipped enough to identify the opportunities in the market? What more we need to do?
39. How big companies with huge investments can affect our opportunities?
40. What can we do to manage any negative impact on us?

41. What are the key success factors (KSFs) for opportunities in our industry?
42. Do we have these KSFs?
43. How can we strengthen these KSFs?

Factors Influencing Sales

Specify the main factors which influence our sales and the reasons for their impact. Describe our strength in predicting the behavior of these factors and strategy to manage our sales within the influence of these factors.

Points for Discussion

1. How can we capture this market?
2. Which companies in our industry are best placed to do it?
3. How many companies are looking forward to make their mark in this market?
4. What are those factors which would increase our sales?
5. How marketing would affect our revenues? How would it affect cost? What is cost-benefit analysis for this?
6. How extensive sales effort would affect our revenues? How would it affect cost? What is cost-benefit analysis for this?
7. How features of our offering would affect our sales figures?
8. How pricing would impact the sales figures of our offering?
9. How the promise of after sales service would impact the sale of products?
10. What are other factors which could increase sales?
11. Can we create differentiation by introducing any other factor in the market?
12. What events generally affect our sales?
13. How can we improve ourselves to capture maximum possible sales of a particular offering in the market without negatively affecting other sales figure?

Opportunity for Niche Market

Describe the opportunity to market our products and services to a niche in the market. Specify our strengths in profitably selling our offerings to this market.

Points for Discussion

1. Can we identify a niche in the market?
2. What are the reasons for this niche? Why it exist?
3. What is the demand of this niche?
4. What offerings could serve this niche?
5. Do our existing offerings can satisfy the demands of this niche?
6. If not, what do we need to develop or offer to serve this niche market?
7. Has other players identified this niche?
8. Can other players enter this niche?
9. How easy or difficult is for other players to enter it?
10. How would that affect us?
11. How can we prepare ourselves for that?
12. How can we create a leadership position in this niche market?
13. What do we need to do for that?
14. Is this any opportunity to build a strong brand in this niche?
15. What do we need to do to build that strong brand?
16. How can we build a strong bond with this niche?
17. Does it make a business sense to create a niche in the market? What is the business case for that?
18. What would we need to do to create this niche in the market?
19. What are the cost implications?
20. What is the dollar value of the niche market?
21. What are the demographic factors of this niche?

22. What other products and services can be offered to this niche?

Our Consumers

Describe the customers and consumers of our products and services. Specify the needs and demands satisfied through our offerings and the reasons for our success in this segment.

Points for Discussion

1. How can we define our target customer segment (TCS)?
2. What need of customers is being satisfied by our offerings?
3. What is their consumption capacity for our offering?
4. What is the worth of each customer i.e. how much business is expected from each customer over a time period?
5. How can we increase her expenditure on our offerings?
6. Can we increase the number of our offerings for this customer segment?
7. What would be the percentage increase of expenditure per customer on our offerings?
8. How do they react to price change?
9. What wrong action from our side can break trust or repulse them?
10. What basic rules we need to always follow to keep this segment satisfied?
11. What actions we should never do?
12. What are the best ways to communicate with them?
13. How do we take their feedback?
14. How can we increase the size of our target customer segment?
15. What are the substitutes available for TCS which they can replace with our offerings?

16. What percentage of TCS uses these substitutes?
17. How can we divert some of these TCS from substitutes to use our offerings?
18. How can we earn more from TCS?
19. What differentiation we offer?
20. How our offerings are positioned?
21. How can we improve our relation with them?

Consumer Perception

Specify the perception of our consumers about our offerings. Describe our efforts to improve this perception consistently.

Points for Discussion

1. How does market perceive our offerings? Is it good or bad?
2. How does it affect our revenues and profitability?
3. How does it affect our brand image?
4. What are the main reasons for this perception?
5. What actions we have taken till now? What are the results of these actions?
6. What can we do to improve this perception?
7. How is this perception in relation to our other offerings?
8. What are the reasons for this difference?
9. How do we get the feedback from market?
10. What is the reliability of this feedback?
11. How often we take feedback from market?
12. How our past records tell us about our action on customer feedback?
13. How our sincerity for solving customer's problems can improve our revenues?
14. What do we need to do to improve our sincerity for customer feedback?
15. What is the difference between our primary feedback about customers and secondary feedback by other researchers like media, consultants etc.?
16. What do they feel about the features of our offerings?
17. What is their experience about using our offerings?
18. Where is the gap?

19. What we need to do to fill the gap in our offerings to completely satisfy our customers within reasonable cost and pricing?
20. How is our price perceived in the market?
21. How can we improve this perception about pricing?
22. Do we have enough margins to reduce our pricing? If not, what is our plan?
23. How government rules and regulations affect our offerings and prices?
24. What can we do about it?
25. How other players in industry manage it?
26. Can we work with industry participants to suggest government about removing wrong rules and regulations?
27. What is the probability of this effort having any effect?
28. Are we ready to keep our business up and strong in any circumstances?

Existing Market

Describe the sources which serve the demand of our customer segment. Specify the main reasons for the shift of target segment towards our products and services.

Points for Discussion

1. How present need is satisfied by the market?
2. What are the products and services which are meeting these needs?
3. Which companies are supplying these products and services to the market?
4. Do customers feel satisfied with these offerings?
5. If not, then what are the reasons for that?
6. Where the gap between what is demanded and what is offered?
7. How this gap will be filled?
8. What we propose to offer to the market?
9. How our offerings would fill this gap?
10. Have we tested it in the market with the Target Customer Segment (TCS)?
11. At what level are the present offerings priced?
12. Is this pricing level acceptable in the market?
13. Is TCS feeling fine about it?
14. How the change in pricing would affect the demand?
15. What is our learning about demanded product and service and their pricing, which would be embraced in the market?
16. What is the total market of the offering? What are the total weekly, monthly sales?
17. Where do we fit in the market?
18. What would be the specifications of our offering?
19. What should be our penetration strategy in the market?

20. What would be our communication strategy?
21. What unique ways can we have to deliver our message to the market?
22. What impact would they have?
23. How can we take consistent feedback from the market to improve?
24. How our brand equity would keep evolving in this market?
25. What is our pricing?
26. Is this pricing acceptable in the market? Is present pricing optimal enough to drive maximum sales?
27. How the market would react to the price change of our offering?
28. How would others players in the industry would react to our offering and pricing?
29. How would that affect us?
30. How is our offering different in features and need satisfaction?
31. How TCS rate it in comparison to other similar offerings in the market?
32. Is our offering good enough to attract users who use substitutes?
33. What strategies other competitors can use to resist our offering?
34. Are new entrants with similar offerings entering the market? How are they performing in the market?
35. How are the offerings of new entrants different from us?
36. Can we learn anything from them?
37. How would their entry affect us?
38. What supporting networks do we need for this offering? Have we set them up?
39. If the existing penetration plan does not work then what is our Plan B?
40. In how much time would we know that the existing plan is not working?

Competitor's Image

Specify the competitor's image in the market and their brand equity for Target Customer Segment. Specify the reasons for the strength of our market image in comparison to competitors.

Points for Discussion

1. How does the market view our competitors?
2. What is the brand image of our competitors for Target Customer Segment (TCS)?
3. Why is this brand image established about competitors? What mistakes or right they did?
4. What can we learn from this analysis?
5. What image does TCS has about us?
6. How can we improve our image?
7. Are we considered better or worse by TCS in comparison to competitors?
8. How can we take advantage of this fact?
9. How can we differentiate from our competitors?
10. How would we identify the differentiating factors for our offerings?
11. What is the process involved in communicating our differentiating factors to TCS?
12. What would be the message for communication?
13. Through which channel would it be delivered?
14. If TCS is satisfied with the current offerings of competitors then what should be our offering?
15. What would be our strategy to penetrate the market?
16. How innovative promotions would be used to connect with TCS?
17. What would be the total earning potential for this offering?
18. What is the cost-benefit-analysis for this offering?

19. Could it better to target other niches and offerings instead of present one for better ROI (Return on Investment)?

Advertising Techniques

Specify the advertising and promotional techniques used by us. Compare them with the techniques used by our competitors. Describe the marketing techniques with maximum impact.

Points for Discussion

1. How do other players of industry advertise?
2. Which channels they use generally? Why they use them?
3. How do they use these channels?
4. Are they innovative in using these channels?
5. What is the effectiveness of these advertisements? How do we measure that effectiveness?
6. How can these advertisements be improved?
7. Which market players are involved in this e.g. media planners, media buyers, content creators, advertising agency etc.?
8. How do these players (advertising) affect the market?
9. What is the average spending of industry on advertising?
10. Who spends maximum on advertising? What is their ROI? Which companies have maximum advertising ROI?
11. What is the optimum amount of marketing required by the market? How can we beat competitors in advertising impact?
12. What is our budgeted amount for advertising?
13. How can we have maximum impact in the market with least expenditure? What should be our strategy?
14. Which channels and methods would be most effective?

15. Which promotional techniques are being used by industry players?
16. Are these promotional techniques innovative?
17. What is the objective of these promotional techniques?
18. What effect these promotions have on TCS?
19. What is the ROI for these promotions?
20. Has the promotion and advertising and promotions grown over the years in this industry? What are the main reasons for that?
21. How has major competitor's investment in advertising & promotion grown over the years? What are the main reasons for that?
22. How the advertising would grow in our industry in coming years? What are the main reasons for that?
23. What should be our strategy to have maximum impact through advertising and promotion in future? How would innovation support us?
24. What are the chances that these efforts would have negative impact? What could be the reasons for that?
25. What are the risks in advertising and promotion strategy for us?
26. How can we mitigate these risks?
27. How fast these innovative ideas in advertising and promotions would be copied by other players?
28. Which advertising strategies are most effective and least effective?
29. What are the reasons for varying effectiveness of advertising strategies?
30. What can we learn from these reasons?
31. What do we interpret about communicating to TCS through advertising and promotion? What strategy impacts them maximum?
32. What can we learn from other industries and markets about the best practices in advertising and promotions?

33. How our advertising efforts affect our brand equity?
34. How can we calculate our advertising and promotions ROI accurately?

Pricing

Specify the pricing for our products and services. Compare them with the pricing of our competitors. Describe the reasons for our products and services optimally priced which would be accepted by our customers and market.

Points for Discussion

1. At what prices our competing products and services are available in the market?
2. How is this pricing compared to ours?
3. How this pricing structure in the market affects us?
4. What is the behavior of Target Customer Segment (TCS) at this pricing structure in the market?
5. Are customers of our offering price sensitive? What are their sensitivity levels?
6. What are the margins in our offerings? What is the industry average?
7. Are these margins sustainable?
8. Which industry players are able to manage maximum margins? How? What can we learn from them?
9. How does prices and features of offering are related to each other? Do prices rise with features?
10. How would be our strategy to manage profitability if costs rise? Would it be fine to increase prices of our offerings in this case? How would it affect our sales figures?
11. What percentage of customers would move to substitutes with price rise? How would that affect us?
12. What would be the pricing strategy of customers with cost rise?
13. How customers define quality for our products and services?

14. What quality of products and services we provide now? How can this quality be increased and decreased?
15. Would TCS accept our offerings at low price with lower quality?
16. How this fact affects our strategy?
17. Can we find innovative ways to cut our prices while keeping the offerings same in quality and features?
18. Which are the main elements of pricing and how do they affect the pricing?
19. Are we clear about each element of pricing with statistical data of their impact on pricing?
20. What can we do to manage them better?
21. Can we increase the number of our offerings, with slight variations in features, serving different niches of TCS? How the pricing would be calculated for each without impact other offering? How would we justify the prices of offerings?
22. If prices seem high, can we add some services with our offerings to justify the prices? Will it be acceptable to TCS?

Competitor's SWOT

Present the SWOT analysis of our competitors. Describe the reasons for our strength in the market in comparison with our competitors.

Points for Discussion

1. What is the SWOT analysis of competitors (Strength, weakness, opportunity, threats)?
2. Are we ready with an in-depth analysis of competitors and our comparison with them?
3. Where each competitor stands on the competitive landscape?
4. How can our competitors be defeated in the marketplace?
5. What are our competitor's major strengths and weaknesses? What can we learn from them?
6. How can we take advantage from competitor's weaknesses?
7. What are competitor's plans about the future?
8. What are the reasons for these plans?
9. What are the competitive advantages of competitors?
10. What are our strategies to face these competitive advantages of competitors?
11. What would be the competitor's strategies against us?
12. What actions do we need to take to neutralize their strategies against us?
13. What are the historical facts about our competitors?
14. How these historical facts would help us in better prediction about competitors?
15. Who are the stars in competitors?

16. What unique is about these stars? What can we learn from them?
17. What is our strategy to face these stars in marketplace?
18. What actions of competitors can increase the heat of competition?
19. What would be our actions during that time?
20. What is their decision making process?
21. Can we predict their future actions?
22. What are our understanding about their mission, vision, goals and strategy?
23. How sincere is their management to pursue their mission?

Competitive Advantage

Specify the competitive advantage of our company and our competitors. Specify our strategy to beat the competitive advantages of our competitors.

Points for Discussion

1. What is our Competitive Advantage?
2. Why is it our Competitive Advantage?
3. How does it differentiate us in marketplace?
4. How does it make us unique and stronger?
5. How can we maintain this Competitive Advantage?
6. How other players react to our Competitive Advantage?
7. What are their strategies to beat our Competitive Advantage?
8. How their actions would affect us?
9. What are our plans to repulse their offence against our Competitive Advantage?
10. What are the associated risks?
11. How can we mitigate them?
12. How can we have more Competitive Advantages?
13. What is required to build new Competitive Advantages?
14. What resources would be required?
15. How can we arrange for these resources?
16. Can we take ideas from other markets and industries?

Competitor's Distribution

Specify the distribution channels used by our competitors. Describe the strengths and weaknesses of these channels.

Points for Discussion

1. What distribution channels are used by our competitors?
2. How their products are delivered?
3. What are their Point of Sales and Points of Distribution?
4. Are these distribution channels of competitors outsourced or owned by competitors? What are the reasons?
5. What is the cost of distribution of each competitor? How is it compared to industry standard?
6. What is the bargaining power of their distribution channels?
7. What are the advantages and disadvantages of each type of distribution?
8. Are customers happy with the distribution of competitors?
9. What are the customer's complaints about competitors?
10. What is our learning from these customer's complaints?
11. How has competitors reacted to the customer's complaints?
12. What are the future distribution plans of competitors?

Distribution Channels

Specify the distribution channels of our company. Describe the reasons of their strength over the competition.

Points for Discussion

1. How do we distribute our products?
2. What are our channels of distribution?
3. How our distribution channels different from competitors?
4. Are our distribution channels common with competitors?
5. How would it affect us?
6. Can we identify better ways to distribute our products?
7. How is our distribution better or worse than competition? Why?
8. How can we improve our distribution?
9. How Customers feels about our distribution?
10. What are customer's complaints against us?
11. How fast we act on customer's complaints?
12. What is our process to resolve customer's complaints?
13. How we have improved over time in distribution?
14. What is our understanding about distribution of products to customers?
15. How can innovation help us in distribution?
16. How do we use technology in distribution?
17. How technology improves the efficiency of distribution?
18. What is ROI of technology in distribution?
19. How do other markets and industries use technology in distribution?
20. What is our cost of distribution?

21. Which reason would compel us to outsource the distribution channel?
22. What are the pros and cons of outsourcing the distribution channel?
23. What are our plans for future to improve our distribution?

Market Connection

Describe the various ways to connect to market and our target segment. Specify the uniqueness of our advertising and promotional techniques.

Points for Discussion

1. How do we connect with the target market?
2. How do we use advertising and promotions?
3. Which advertising modes are used by us? Why?
4. What are the types of promotions we use? Why?
5. How is our adverting and promotions different from competitors?
6. How effective are we in attracting the attention of target segment?
7. What is the ROI of advertising?
8. What is our image in the market?
9. Do we have brand recognition?
10. What is our brand equity?
11. How can we build better company and product brands?
12. How is our brand ranked in the market?
13. How customers perceive us?
14. How creative are we in communicating our brand message?
15. How effective are our communication messages?
16. What is our frequency of communication to market?
17. Why is this frequency right?
18. What can we learn from other strong brands and companies about brand building?

Marketing Mix

Describe the marketing mix of our company and compare it with competitors. Specify the reasons for its effectiveness in the market.

Points for Discussion

1. How are our products and services sold?
2. What is the role of sales team in product sales?
3. How does marketing and sales team coordinate to create strategies and plans?
4. What are the key result areas for marketing and sales teams? How are they calculated?
5. Does our present sale meet the target?
6. If no, what are the reasons for low sales?
7. How can we improve our sales?
8. What wrong are we doing in sales and marketing?
9. How can we find faults in our sales and marketing?
10. How is our sale in comparison to other competitors?
11. How can we change our marketing mix to have better impact in the market?
12. What indications do we get from scenario analysis?
13. How flexible is our company to change with the market?
14. How competitors handle the changes in the market?
15. How our marketing mix would affect our brand?
16. What primary marketing research have we done?
17. Which secondary marketing data is available to us?
18. How reliable is this data? Can we take decisions based upon this data?
19. How can we differentiate in the market without increasing cost and negatively impacting our brand?

Marketing Program

Describe our marketing program to carry out our marketing strategy. Specify the reasons for its effectiveness.

Points for Discussion

1. What is our marketing plan?
2. How was marketing plan developed?
3. Who takes the complete responsibility of this plan?
4. How is our marketing plan different from other major players in the market?
5. What impact is expected from this plan?
6. How would we calculate the impact of marketing plan?
7. How the plan and its execution could be modified?

Marketing Strategy Analysis

Specify our marketing strategy. Analyze it holistically to prove its strength and effectiveness in the market. Check the marketing strategy of each of the competitor and analyze it for its strength and weaknesses.

Points for Discussion

1. What primary demographic trends pose threats and opportunities for our company?
2. What developments in income, prices, savings and credit will have impact on the company?
3. What is the outlook for costs and availability of natural resources and energy? Is the company environmentally responsible?
4. What technological changes are occurring? What is the company's position on technology?
5. What current and proposed laws will affect company strategy?
6. What is the public's attitude towards business and the company's products? What changes in consumer lifestyles might have an impact?
7. What is happening to market size, growth, geographic distribution and profits? Which are the large market segments?
8. How do customers rate the company on product quality, service and price? How do they make their buying decisions?
9. Who are the chief competitors? What are their strategies, market shares, and strengths and weaknesses?
10. Which main channels does the company use to distribute products to customers? How are they performing?

11. What trends are affecting suppliers? What is the outlook for the availability of key production resources?
12. Which key trends provide problems or opportunities? How should the company deal with these trends?
13. Is the mission clearly defined and market-oriented?
14. Has the company set clear objectives to guide marketing planning and performance? Do these objectives fit with the company's opportunities and strengths?
15. Does the company have a sound marketing strategy for achieving its objectives?
16. Has the company budgeted sufficient resources to segments, products, territories and marketing-mix elements?
17. Does the chief marketing officer have adequate authority over activities affecting customer satisfaction?
18. Are activities optimally structured along functional, product, market and territory lines?
19. Do marketing, sales and other staff communicate effectively? Is the staff well trained, supervised, motivated and evaluated?
20. Does staff work well across functions: marketing with manufacturing, R & D, buying, personnel, etc.?
21. Is the marketing intelligence system providing accurate and timely information about developments? Are decision makers using marketing research effectively?
22. Does the company prepare annual, long-term and strategic plans? Are they used effectively?
23. Are annual plan objectives being achieved? Does management periodically analyze the sales and profitability of products, markets, territories and channels?

24. Is the company well organized to gather, generate and screen new product ideas? Does it carry out adequate product and market testing? Has the company succeeded with new products?
25. How profitable are the company's different products, markets, territories and channels? Should the company enter, expand or withdraw from any business segments? What would he the consequences?
26. Do any activities have excessive costs? How can costs be reduced?
27. Has the company developed sound product-line objectives? Should some products be phased out? Should some new products he added? Would some products benefit from quality, style or feature changes?
28. What are the company's pricing objectives, policies, strategies and procedures? Arc the company's prices in line with customer's perceived value? Are price promotions used properly?
29. What are the distribution objectives and strategies? Does the company have adequate market coverage and service? Should existing channels be changed or new ones added?
30. What are the company's promotional objectives?
31. How is the budget determined? Is it sufficient? Are advertising messages and media channels well developed and are received by market? Does the company have well-developed sales promotion and public relations programs?
32. What are the company's sales force objectives? Is the sales force large enough? Is it properly organized? Is it well trained, supervised and motivated? How is the sales force rated relative to those of competitors?

Revenue Targets

Specify the company's targets for revenue and profitability. Describe the logic and reasons for these targets. Specify our plan to meet these targets.

Points for Discussion

1. What are our sales and profit goals?
2. What are the reasons to set these goals?
3. How are these goals in comparison to other players of industry?
4. How are these plans in sync with our mission?
5. What is required to achieve these goals?
6. What is our margin percentage?
7. What major reasons would affect sales and profits of our company?
8. Which of these reasons are external and internal?
9. How can we control these internal reasons?
10. How can we manage ourselves among external factors?
11. What is our strategy to achieve these goals?
12. What are forecast sales for the company for each of the next twelve months and for each of the next three years?

Promotional Strategy

Specify the promotional strategy of our company and describe its strength and uniqueness in the market.

Points for Discussion

1. What are our sales targets for next three years?
2. What selling strategy and techniques will be used to achieve required sales targets?
3. What is the demand, needs and expectations of the target customer group?
4. Is target market aware about our company, brand and offering? If not, what do we need to do to inform them?
5. How we educate our customer segment about our offerings?
6. What is our promotional strategy and methodology?
7. What message can be used to persuade the target customer group that the company can meet their needs and demands?

THE OPERATING PLAN

Value Proposition

Specify the value proposition of the company's products and services to the market. Describe the ways we employ to improve our value proposition consistently.

Points for Discussion

1. What is the value proposition of the company?
2. Is this value proposition unique?
3. How is value created?
4. How is it valued by the market?
5. What resources are used in creating value?
6. How are we able to source these resources?
7. Where is value created?
8. How does the location affect the value proposition?
9. How do operations contribute to the company's success?
10. What factors influence operations?
11. How are we able to manage these factors?
12. How the location of company, market, vendors and skills supply does affects our operations?
13. How logistics and government regulations affect our business operations?
14. How other macro factors like political, economic and social impacts our revenues and profits?

Location

Specify the location of our company. Describe the reasons for choosing this location.

Points for Discussion

1. What is the location of business?
2. Why this location was chosen?
3. How and why this location contribute to the success of the business?
4. What competitive advantages does this location offers?
5. What is the real-estate cost of the location?
6. What benefits does the government provide at this location?
7. How is the supply of skilled labor at this location?
8. Can our employees settle at this location?
9. How are the transportation facilities at this location?
10. Is this location easily accessible to our suppliers?
11. Are we easily able to meet our inventory needs?
12. What is the status of energy availability at the location?
13. What is the tax structure at the location?
14. Is our location has convenient access to market and customers?
15. What would be the distribution costs from the location?
16. How product perishability can be managed from the location?
17. Can we implement world class manufacturing practices?
18. Do we have required customer demand to support the business?

19. Does this geographical location has sufficient purchasing power to generate desired sales for us?
20. Is our point of sale is motivating enough to close sales?
21. Do we have enough support of the industry clusters?
22. What is our cluster analysis for our industry and supporting sectors?

Operations Plan - Manufacturing

Describe the operations of the manufacturing company.

Points for Discussion

1. What are the products offered to the market by the company?
2. What is the output data of the company? How is it in relation to industry average?
3. What is the output data at full capacity of production?
4. What machinery and equipment are required for production in our company?
5. What is the productivity of our manufacturing operations?
6. How can we improve our productivity?
7. What are the major stages of our production process?
8. What is the work flow? Why is this workflow efficient?
9. What value is added to the product at each stage of production?
10. What raw materials are required to manufacture the product?
11. What is the cost of each activity?
12. How price variations of raw materials affect our cost and prices?
13. What skills –set is required for production?
14. What is our personnel cost? How does it rise each year?
15. What is the material and labor cost per unit of output?
16. How can we make our production process as our competitive advantage?

17. What are the "key success factors" for production process?
18. How does production process contribute to the overall success of the business?
19. What are the best processes and practices we use in manufacturing? How do they help us in reducing costs and improving productivity?
20. What technology do we use in production?
21. How does technology help us to improve our production?
22. What processes we have outsourced?
23. How outsourcing helps us in our business?
24. How the sub-components are sourced? Can we find better ways for sourcing sub-components?
25. How is production volume decided? What is the process involved in it? What are the advantages for using this process?
26. Is our production process labor intensive or capital intensive?
27. What are our overheads?
28. How do we calculate our activity wise production costs?
29. What is the ratio of fixed and variable costs? How does it affect our cost management?
30. What is our breakeven volume?
31. How do we manage our costs?

Operations Plan - Services

Describe the operations plans for a services company

Points for Discussion

1. What services do we offer to market?
2. What is required to offer these services?
3. What demand and need it satisfies in the market?
4. What are the various stages to provide the service?
5. What steps are involved at each stage of providing the service?
6. What are the key success factors for our service?
7. How can we make our services as our competitive advantage?
8. What is the performance of our services?
9. How our services are rated by customers?
10. Do we outsource a part of our services?
11. How do we calculate the costs of providing the services?
12. What skills are required to provide the services?
13. How do we source this skill set?
14. What is our personnel cost to provide the service?
15. What assurances do we give to our consumers about services?
16. What are our fixed and variable costs?
17. What are the ratios for fixed and variable costs?
18. What is the optimum ratio for fixed and variable costs?
19. How can we improve our cost ratio?
20. What are our profit margins?
21. How can we maintain these margins?
22. What is the breakeven level of the service revenue of the company
23. How do we measure and maintain our costs for providing the services?

Operation Design

Describe the layout and operating facilities for production.

Points for Discussion

1. How do we manage the production of planned output?
2. Do we own the production facility or have we leased it? What are the pro and cons for each?
3. What are the risks associated with ownership and leasing the facilities?
4. How can we manage these risks?
5. What is the requirement of physical space to carry out our operations?
6. What special characteristics would be required for physical space?
7. What are our requirements for space for inventory management?
8. What supporting assets are required for production?
9. How can machines and workers coordinate with each other for improving efficiency?
10. What are the main features of our operating facilities which can provide competitive advantage to us?
11. How do we measure our costs?
12. How can we manage our costs?
13. What is the contribution of operation facilities to the success of our business?
14. What is the maintenance cost of plant and machinery? How is it in comparison to industry?
15. What is the average life of our crucial machinery and assets?

16. Where do we stand in comparison to other players of industry?
17. How the design of our production is better than our competitors? How can we maintain this edge?
18. Are our assets insured? Which insurance plan covers our assets? What are the reasons for taking the particular insurance plan?
19. How do we control and ensure the efficiency of our work-flow?
20. Do our processes and procedures meet the government standards?

Purchasing

Describe purchasing procedures followed by our company. Specify the reasons for their effectiveness to procure the best material at lowest cost.

Points for Discussion

1. What is the purchase policy of our company?
2. What are the reasons to create this policy?
3. Which purchases are critical to the company's operation and why?
4. How the purchase is initiated? Is it automatic or initiated by managers?
5. How the quantity is calculated?
6. How the purchase is authorized?
7. Who has the authority to place the purchase?
8. What is the vendor selection process?
9. How the quality of the material to be bought is decided?
10. How the pricing is decided?
11. How the quality and quantity of the material received by our company is checked?
12. What is the vendor selection process?
13. What are the main criteria which influences this process?
14. What is the credit period we demand from vendors? How this credit period is in comparison to industry?
15. Do we have multiple vendors for key items?
16. Do we have alternative sources of supply of material?
17. How reliable are our suppliers in terms of product availability, meeting lead time, service and quality control?

18. If our vendors are unreliable then what are our contingency plans to ensure the supply of raw materials?
19. What is the ratio of purchasing cost and total operating cost?
20. How do we manage purchasing cost?
21. How the purchasing order is tracked?
22. How do we manage purchasing records and how do we archive them?
23. How can purchasing function be our competitive advantage?
24. How do we ensure that the payment to vendors is smooth and without delays?
25. What other methods are available to improve our purchasing by improving efficiency and reducing cost?

Inventory Management

Describe the inventory management techniques and procedures of our company. Specify the reasons for their effectiveness in relation to other players in the industry.

Points for Discussion

1. How inventory needs are projected?
2. How inventory projections are related to sales projections?
3. Which is considered as the critical inventory for our business?
4. What is the average daily usage or sales rate of the key inventory items?
5. What is material-wise minimum level of inventory to conduct operations properly and to avoid disrupting production or losing sales?
6. How do we determine the minimum level of inventory for each item and component?
7. How purchasing is linked with inventory management?
8. How the purchase order is triggered if minimum inventory level is reached?
9. How do we manage this triggering process?
10. How do we utilize modern communication technologies to improve processes and procedures by taking better decisions?
11. Which are the major costs in inventory management?
12. How do we monitor and manage inventory costs?
13. How inventory is managed and utilized in best possible way to improve productivity and reducing costs?
14. How technology is used in inventory management?

15. How technology makes inventory management more efficient?
16. How the inventory management is reviewed by the management?
17. How inventory thefts are prevented? What methods are used?
18. How our inventory management and control is one of the most effective system in industry?
19. How inventory management can act as our competitive advantage?

Quality Control

Specify the procedures for managing quality of products and other operating procedures. Describe the processes for serving the customers and ensuring their satisfaction.

Points for Discussion

1. What principles and policies we follow to ensure an acceptable level of quality and customer satisfaction?
2. How these principles and policies are communicated to company employees and staff?
3. How do we establish the quality standards?
4. How do we develop execution plans for these quality standards?
5. How do we execute these quality standards?
6. How do we measure our products and services against these quality standards?
7. How do we establish customer satisfaction standards?
8. How do we execute our customer satisfaction standards?
9. How are our quality standards and customer satisfaction standards in comparison to industry?
10. How these standards would give us competitive advantage I the market?
11. How we analyze the customer attitude about product quality and services?
12. How do we determine the customer service needs?
13. How the required information about these standards is generated and used?
14. How do we make sure the quality of delivery from point-of-sale to point-of-delivery?
15. How do we reduce our delivery time while maintain quality?

16. How do we take customer feedback?
17. What is the percentage of rejected products? What are the main reasons for these rejections?
18. How do we manage these rejections to maintain customer satisfaction?
19. How the costs related to maintaining quality control and customer satisfaction?
20. What is our ROI on these costs?

ORGANIZATION PLAN

Management philosophy

Describe the management philosophy of our company. Describe the ways it is used to help us in decision making.

Points for Discussion

1. How the mission of the company is interpreted by all stakeholders?
2. Are they getting the same message? If not, how can we make sure that they get the same understanding of the purpose of the existence of the company?
3. How does it help us in defining the goals of the company, both short term and long term?
4. What is the process of defining goals?
5. How our mission defines values of the company?
6. What is the culture of our company?
7. How do we make sure that this culture is maintained?
8. How this culture would take us towards our mission?
9. Can we find any way in which our values and culture are not in sync with our mission?
10. What can we do to correct it?
11. How the right and wrong is decided in our company?
12. How the decisions are taken in our company?
13. How our mission guides managers in taking decisions?
14. How trade-offs are made in our company?
15. Is our mission and purpose clear to all stakeholders of company?
16. How does mission helps to set goals for various departments and levels?
17. Does the lowest level employee understands her goals and how are they related to mission?
18. How the CSR (Corporate Social Responsibility) policy of the company is decided?
19. How sincere is our team for CSR? What value have we added to society in recent time?

20. What our company stands for?
21. Are we clear about the activities which we will never do?
22. Is every employee in our company clear about her goals and KRAs (Key Result Areas)?
23. How is business managed in our company? What management philosophy we use for taking decisions and actions?
24. How the new ideas of products and services are conceived?
25. How the new products and services are developed and tested? Is this process efficient and effective?
26. What is the recruitment process?
27. What are the main criteria for recruitment?
28. How the retention of employees is managed in our company?
29. Are we clear about the reasons which would make the work satisfactory for each employee?
30. How do we make sure that the personal goal of every employee is matched with organizational goals? Is it maintained consistently?
31. What is the appraisal process of the company?
32. What are the main criteria of promotion and pay increment? How does it motivate employees?
33. What are the main reasons for firing employees? How many were fired in recent time? Why?
34. How do we make sure that our business processes keep improving? What methods do we use?
35. How do we measure the efficiency of business processes?
36. How do we make sure that the productivity of employees keep improving? Which are the tools and methods used by us?
37. Have we created the systems which would capture the ideas of employees about offerings and improvements?
38. How do we evaluate these ideas for implementation?
39. How open are we to criticism by our stakeholders?

40. Is management open to new technologies? How new technologies are evaluated?
41. How is the new technology implemented in company?
42. How do we experiment with new ideas and offerings?
43. How do we finalize products and services for launch?
44. Is management really concerned about customers and their satisfaction?
45. How does management make sure that they receive regular feedback from customers?
46. How the feedback from customers is analyzed and acted upon?
47. How the priorities are set during tough times?
48. During business crisis how the costs are cut, who bears the maximum burden?
49. What is most appreciated and disliked by management? Why?
50. How the local, national and business media view our company and brand?
51. What we need to do to improve our image further in market?
52. How do the actions of top management tell us about their philosophy?
53. What is the process of rewarding the employees?
54. What support and benefits we provide to employees?
55. How are these benefits in comparison to our and other industries?
56. How employees view these benefits?
57. How employees feel about the company and management?
58. How do our employees rate their job-satisfaction on the scale of 10?
59. How do we make sure that our decisions are legal, moral and ethical?

Organization structure

Describe the Organization Structure of the company. Specify the reasons for the design of organization structure and its effect in creating the required management system in our company.

Points for Discussion

1. What is our Organizational Structure (OS)?
2. How OS is designed?
3. What is the purpose of this design of OS?
4. How can we say that this design would be the most effective one for our company?
5. How the communication flows in this OS?
6. How decisions flow in this OS?
7. How the responsibilities are decided for each employee? Are these clear to everybody?
8. What is the KRA (Key Result Areas) for each designation?
9. How are KRAs decided and how are they measured?
10. How promotion and pay rise is decided?
11. Which major factors are looked into for promotion and pay rise of employees?
12. What is our reporting structure? How is it most efficient and effective?
13. Does junior staff get any confusion about reporting?
14. How different departments interact and cooperate with each other?
15. How communication is recorded between employees and departments?
16. How conflicts are resolved?
17. How authority is divided?
18. How our OS support in development and implementation of new ideas?

19. What are the top level management positions in the company?
20. What are the staff and middle level positions in the company?
21. What are the specific duties and responsibilities associated with each management and staff position?
22. What decisions must be made to fulfill the duties and responsibilities associated with each management positions?
23. What number of immediate, lower level subordinates can effectively be supervised by each management and staff positions?
24. What level of authority is assigned to each management and staff positions?
25. Who holds each management position?
26. How effectively does each management and staff position holder delegates' authority to immediate, lower level subordinate?
27. What are the major work units or departments into which the company's primary task can be best divided and re-grouped?
28. How many supervisors are required for each major work unit or department?
29. What duties, responsibilities, and level of authority are associated with each supervisory position?

Compensation and Incentives

Specify the remuneration for the staff and the reasons for these decisions. Describe the plan to attract the best talent in the industry to achieve the projected growth targets.

Points for Discussion

1. What is the designation for each position?
2. What is the objective of each position and what are their responsibilities?
3. What are the tasks assigned to each position?
4. What decision making authority is associated with each position?
5. What education qualifications and competencies are required for each position?
6. What soft and hard skills are required for each position?
7. What attitude and behavioral characteristics are required for each position?
8. What training would be required for each position?
9. How would that training be provided? What would be the cost associated with training?
10. What tools, materials and equipment would be used by each position?
11. How job targets are decided for each job?
12. How the task related deadlines are decided?
13. On average, how many workers are managed by each manager?
14. What are the physical risks associated with complex tasks in our company? How do we manage these risks?
15. Are we following all required standards of government and regulators?
16. What is the cost-to-company associated with each position?

17. What returns do we expect from each position?
18. Are the pay levels enough to attract the talent from industry?
19. What other monetary and non-monetary incentives we provide to each job?
20. What is our recruitment process? How is it better than our competitors?
21. What career path does our company offer?

THE FINANCIAL PLAN

Financing Summary

Specify the summary of the financing required for our company.

1. What amount of financing is needed to make plans feasible?
2. When and in what amounts will the financing be needed?
3. In what form will the financing be needed?
4. Who will provide this financing?

Costing

Specify the costs of our company. Describe our various ways to manage them effectively.

Points for Discussion

1. What are the costs of the company? Which are the major ones?
2. Are we sure that we have identified all costs heads? What are those cost heads?
3. Have we checked these cost heads from the standard templates or financial sheets of industry?
4. What is the meaning of each cost head? How each cost head is adding value?
5. How the numbers of these cost heads are in comparison with other players? Do we have more or less?
6. Do we feel that each cost is delivering relevant value?
7. How have we forecasted our costs for projected financials?
8. How have we calculated the costs for each year?
9. Is this cost on conservative side or inflated side? Why? How can we say that?
10. If inflated cost, what is the expected percentage of inflation of costs in relation to actuals?
11. What is the purpose of inflation of costs?
12. Do specified costs look logical and reasonable?
13. What are the different ways to reduce costs?
14. How latest management and operational practices can reduce costs?
15. How can technology help us to reduce costs?
16. What is the cost benefit analysis of use these latest practices and technologies?
17. Do we have any other ways and methods to reduce costs?
18. How the main players of industry reduce their costs?

19. What is required to implement each of these cost reduction methods?
20. Are we presently using any of these? Which are those? Why?
21. Which methods are not used by us? Why?
22. Are we able to evolve ways to reduce costs?
23. Are we making sure that any reduction in costs would not lead to any reduction in quality and productivity of the company?
24. How can we use innovative technologies to get the competitive advantage by reducing cost and improving productivity and efficiency of processes?
25. Can we go ahead of the normal curve of the industry, so that other players of industry follow us in adopting innovative techniques and technologies?
26. How our costs are in comparison to industry leaders? Can we learn anything from them?
27. Are there other players which manage costs better than us? Can we learn anything from these companies?
28. Which accounting practices are we following?
29. How different accounting practices affect our costing and profitability?
30. For international business how do we need to change our accounting practices? What would be the cost involved in it?
31. How do we calculate depreciation? What is the reason to use the particular method to calculate depreciation? What is our industry practice?
32. How various internal and external factors affect costs? Which are these factors and how and why they affect our costs?
33. How can we control these internal factors?
34. How can we manage ourselves with external factors?
35. What are the risks of increasing costs? Which of these are major ones?
36. How can we mitigate these risks?

37. Is the risk mitigation plan can be improved in any way? Can we get ideas from other industries and markets?
38. Are we prepared to manage risks, if the need arise?
39. How the costs are changing over time? What are the main reasons for these changes?
40. What is the history of annual cost increase in industry? What were the main reasons for that?
41. What is our annual cost increase? What were the main reasons for that increase?
42. What is the activity based increase of costs?
43. Has the cost decreased for few activities? What are the reasons for that decrease?
44. What statistical and other tools we use for the calculation of costs?
45. How do we measure and calculate the increase in costs?
46. For how many years we have predicted the costs of business? What are the reasons for the number of years?
47. What is the probability of accuracy attached with each forecasted year of costs? How we have calculated these probabilities?
48. How the required facts and data are generated? What are the major sources for that? How many are primary sources and secondary sources?
49. What is the reliability of these sources?
50. Are we using free sources of data? Are they reliable?
51. Are we managing our costs in the right, smart and intelligent ways? How can we say that with confidence?
52. How are our management practices in comparison to industry?
53. Can we learn something from other industries about cost management in better ways?
54. How do we calculate the costs of each process?
55. Is this calculation methodology best and most accurate available? If not, why are we using this methodology?
56. Have we checked properly that we are not double counting the costs in any way?

57. Which are variable and fixed costs?
58. Which are the major components of fixed and variable costs?
59. What can we do to reduce the size of major cost components, without affecting the quality and productivity?
60. What can increase the size of the major cost components?
61. How are these related to each other?
62. What should be optimum ratio of fixed and variable cost for our company and industry?
63. Which cost is bigger in size? How does that affect us?
64. How can we have the optimum ratio of fixed and variable costs for every area? How does it affect our plans?
65. What is the right way to manage the costs?
66. What is the optimum level of personnel cost, enough to have good quality workers at least costs? What is our strategy to maintain that level?
67. How do Government rules and regulations affect the costs?
68. What major decisions in business can increase or decrease the costs? In what ways we need to be careful about taking these decisions?
69. Can we consider the outsourcing of non-core business processes?
70. Have we done a proper scenario analysis to forecast future costs?
71. Are we ready for any eventuality to keep our business running and profitable?
72. How does general technology landscape of the market is affecting the costs? Are costs increasing or decreasing?
73. What are the cost centers of the company? Are we managing them properly for required productivity?

74. What could be our unplanned expenditures? Based upon experience and historical analysis, what is the estimated size of these expenditures?
75. How these unplanned expenditures affect our business?
76. How do we plan to meet these unplanned expenditures?
77. What can we learn from history of industry about managing and meeting these unplanned expenditures?
78. What is the probability attached to each of unplanned expenditure? What are the reasons of these probabilities?
79. How can we reduce these probabilities of unplanned expenditures?

Costs Heads

- Describe your marketing, advertising and promotional costs.
- Specify your operational costs, which include all costs related to production of our offerings.
- Specify admiration costs, which include all support functions of our company.
- Specify personnel costs, which include all costs related to company employees.
- Specify miscellaneous cost, which includes all other remaining and contingent costs.
- Specify fixed and variable costs for each cost head. Describe the factors influencing the variable costs.

Costs Assumptions

Specify the assumptions used to calculate the costs. Describe the reasons for choosing these assumptions and their probabilities.

Points for Discussion

1. What are our assumptions to calculate the costs?
2. What is the logic behind taking these assumptions?
3. Have we made sure that our cost calculation is not too much dependent on assumptions?
4. What is the impact of each assumption on out cost calculations?
5. How does our cost plan changes with the changes in each assumption?
6. How big is this change?
7. How our risk analysis and risk management changes with cost plan change due to assumptions?
8. How have our assumptions performed in past? Do we have some real cases to prove that?
9. How many assumptions do we have in comparisons to facts to calculate costs? Our objective should be to have fewer assumptions and more facts.
10. How would we keep improving the accuracy of our proposed cost sheet, with time, as more assumptions are replaced with facts?
11. How can we reduce the number of assumptions?
12. What are the facts which are leading to assumptions?
13. Are we careful about being too optimistic about assumptions?
14. How the variance in assumptions is affecting the fundamentals of Business Plan?
15. Have we considered most of the possible scenarios and assumptions?

16. Have we compared the assumptions with the industry average and major players?

Revenues

Specify the revenues and its sources of our company. Describe the reasons influencing our revenue figures.

Points for Discussion

1. What the sources of revenue?
2. Which are the main revenue sources?
3. What is the pricing of our products and services?
4. How have we arrived at this pricing?
5. How is our pricing in comparison to other industry players and their offerings?
6. How do customers categorize our pricing? Do they find value for their money for our offerings?
7. What is our margin for each product and service?
8. How much extra market is ready to pay for the brand equity of out offerings?
9. How do customers react to the price changes?
10. How any price change of our offerings would impact our revenues and market share?
11. How many revenue streams do we have?
12. Are these revenue streams logical and workable?
13. How each revenue stream is related to other? Are they adding value to each other or overlapping? Can we make them better?
14. Have we missed any revenue stream, which could be offered to the market with minimal efforts? What is the cost-benefit-analysis of this stream?
15. Are all our revenue streams efficient or do we need to remove any which is not adding enough value but increasing cost and efforts?
16. How money is received and collected from customers?
17. Do we offer any credit period to customers? What is that? How does it impact us?

18. What are lost revenues?
19. Do we have any leakage or wastage which is also contributing to lost revenues? How can we stop that leakage and wastage?
20. What actions have we taken to recover our lost revenues? What are the results and success ratio? How can we improve them?
21. How our lost revenue is in comparison to other players of industry?
22. How these players recover their lost revenues? What is their success ratio?
23. How do we feel about increasing our revenues? Is it optimistic or pessimistic? Is it through increasing sales or increasing prices?
24. How would the market react to these changes?
25. How is this optimism for increasing revenues in comparison to industry? Can we do better?
26. What actions do we need to take to increase our revenues?
27. For our company what is the right way of selling more either at low margins or selling less at higher margins?
28. What is our confidence level for these methods?
29. What do we need to take to each to implement?
30. How do customers feel about our offerings? Can they replace us with some other provider of product or service?
31. What is the price band of our offerings in the market? What is our sale at each price level?
32. What can lead to any reduction of our revenues? What would be the main reasons?
33. How can these reasons be managed? Which of these cannot be managed? What can we do about these reasons? How can we prepare ourselves to tackle these reasons?
34. What impacts our increase in revenues – focus on sales or focus on marketing? Why?

35. What can we do to make the weaker one of these have more impact? How much this would add to revenues?
36. If we increase the number of our offerings would it lead to increase in revenues?
37. What can be those offerings?
38. What is the cost-benefit-analysis of these offerings?
39. Is this plan is sync with our strategy and vision? If yes, why this plan is being implemented so late?
40. Are we missing anything which would add to our revenues? Can we get ideas from other markets?
41. If we identity any new offering, what is the process to develop and commercialize it?

Revenue Assumptions

Specify the assumptions used to calculate the costs. Describe the reasons for choosing these assumptions and their probabilities.

Points for Discussion

1. What are the assumptions to calculate the revenues?
2. What is the logic behind taking these assumptions?
3. Have we made sure that our revenue calculation is not too much dependent on assumptions?
4. What is the impact of each assumption on out revenue calculations?
5. How does our revenue plan changes with the changes in each assumption?
6. How big is this change?
7. How our risk analysis and risk management changes with revenue plan change due to assumptions?
8. How have our assumptions performed in past? Do we have some real cases to prove that performance?
9. How many assumptions do we have in comparisons to facts to calculate revenues? Our objective should be to have fewer assumptions and more facts?
10. How would we keep improving the accuracy of our proposed revenue sheet, with time, as more assumptions are replaced by facts?
11. How can we reduce the number of assumptions?
12. What are the facts which are leading to assumptions?
13. Are we careful about being too optimistic about assumptions?
14. How the variance in assumptions is affecting the fundamentals of Business Plan?
15. Have we considered most of the possible scenarios and assumptions?

16. Have we compared the assumptions with the industry average and major players?

Profits & Loss

Describe the Profit and Loss calculations for our company.

Points for Discussion

1. Is the forecast of profit and loss optimistic or pessimistic?
2. What are the main reasons for this optimism and pessimism?
3. How is industry faring during this forecasted period?
4. How is it in comparison to past performance of our company?
5. What would lead to loss or low profit?
6. What could be the reasons for high cost and low revenues?
7. Have we analyzed all reasons in detail?
8. What can we do about these reasons? What actions can we take?
9. What can lead to higher profits?
10. How can we maintain these higher profits?
11. How in other ways would increase in profitability affect our company e.g. employee motivation?
12. Which tax policies apply to us?
13. What are the exemptions in the taxes which apply to us?
14. What is our interest cost? How is it in comparison to industry average?
15. How can our interest cost be reduced?
16. What should we do to keep interest cost low?
17. What is our debt/equity ratio? How is it in comparison to other players of industry?
18. How much money do we require now to execute our business plans?
19. What are the various sources to raise money?

20. What are the different ways to raise the money?
21. Which method of raising money would be most suitable to us?
22. What would be required from our side to raise money?
23. Are we ready with those requirements? If not, what we need to do to arrange those requirements?
24. When would we able to self-sustain ourselves?
25. How can we increase our profitability to maximum?
26. What steps are we taking to increase our profitability?
27. How can we manage these steps?
28. Are our projections of profits reasonable?
29. What would make these projections look unreasonable? Are we careful about those reasons?
30. Do we have logical reasoning to convince potential investors about these projections?
31. What impression our profit plan would leave on investors?
32. How our profit plan would help investors to multiply their money?
33. What are the reasons that would make her invest money in our company?
34. Will we put all our savings in this company with the hope to multiply our money?
35. If the profit plan is not met then how are we going to sustain ourselves?
36. What could be the major events (with high probability of happening) which can change everything for better? Are we ready to capture this potential opportunity?
37. How other players in the industry are performing in term of profitability?
38. How is it in comparison to us?
39. What can we learn from their experiences? Which of these learning are implementable? What we actions do we need to take for that?
40. How all this would affect our brand equity? Is it negative or positive?
41. In what ways we can enhance our brand equity?

42. How should we make sure that any of our actions do not affect our brand equity negatively?
43. What are the main factors which would support us in improving and sustaining profits?
44. What is or main focus area – profitability or market share?
45. How would profitability be affected if we focus on market share and vice versa?
46. What is the size of our cash reserves?
47. What is our plan to use this cash reserve which would add maximum value to us?
48. Have we considered all scenarios of using our cash reserves?
49. Financially, is our strategy working well? How can we say that?
50. If not, what we need to do to correct it?
51. What process would be involved in this correction process? How would it impact us?
52. How are we sure that the new strategy would work for us?
53. What is our process of forecasting?
54. What is our prediction about our profitability for next five years?
55. What is our confidence level for this prediction?
56. What actions do we need to take to up with this profitability prediction?
57. What gaps do we need to fill to achieve this profitability?

Balance Sheet

Present the balance sheet of the company. Describe the reasons for financial decisions.

Points for Discussion

1. How much external financing must be raised to support anticipated growth during the planning period?
2. What category of financing we need to use? Why?
3. What would be the form (debt or equity) of financing?
4. What is the maximum percentage of debt financing which we can use?
5. How the emergency funds would be raised?
6. Who would be our target investors? Who can help us to raise this financing?
7. What is our previous financial performance? How is it compared to industry?
8. What is our current financial performance? How is it compared to industry?
9. What are our financial projections, monthly and annually?
10. What are the financial projections of our competitors?
11. What are our plans to achieve these financial goals?
12. How do we manage our progress towards these financial goals?
13. How our monthly sale is divided into cash and credit?
14. What is our average level of inventory purchase based on sales forecast?
15. What is our credit period for our suppliers?
16. What are our cash expenses for each month?
17. What are our reserves for unforeseen emergencies?

18. Which financing sources can realistically provide us this financing?

Cash Flow

Describe the cash flow situation of our company. Specify the projected cash-flow for our company.

Points for Discussion

1. What is the expected cash flow for this year?
2. Does this cash flow show problems? Why these problems exist?
3. How are we going to solve these problems?
4. What is our prediction of cash flow for next three to five years? Is it negative anywhere?
5. What is our plan to face negative cash flow?
6. What is our level of ease for cash flow for each time period?
7. What we need to do to reach to that level of cash flow?
8. If we are not able to achieve that level of ease then how is it going to affect us?
9. What are the risks associated with weak cash flow?
10. How are we going to manage these risks?
11. What are the other sources of money if the defined sources do not work?
12. Do we have enough buffers of reserves to meet any emergency or unplanned expenditure?
13. What are the other sources of money to meet unplanned expenditures?
14. What we need to do to be able to raise money fast, if required for emergencies?
15. What are the various ways to raise that?
16. Do we have ready sources to raise debt fast, if required?
17. Are we ready with the required formalities to raise debt?

18. Do we have a better way to raise money? Have we explored all possible options?
19. How money is raised by other players of the market?
20. What are their main reasons to choose these sources?
21. Can we learn something from their experiences and plans?
22. How other industries raise money? Can we learn something from them?
23. What are our main practices to manage the cash?

Valuation

Specify the expected valuation of our company. Describe the various ways we can use to improve this valuation.

Points for Discussion

1. What is the present ownership structure of our company?
2. How would this structure look after raising funds?
3. What is the owner's investment in the company?
4. What is the history of valuation and funds raised?
5. What is the expected valuation of our company?
6. How we have arrived at this valuation?
7. What are the main reasons for this valuation?
8. What is the contribution of intangibles to this valuation?
9. What factors are contributing for high valuation? Can we improve upon these factors?
10. Which factors are pulling it down? What can we do about these factors?
11. What methodology we have used to arrive at this valuation?
12. What is the valuation of our company by using other methods?
13. What are the reasons to choose the specific method for calculation of our company's valuation?
14. Can someone prove it wrong?
15. Which reasons can someone specify to prove it wrong?
16. How can we counter those reasons which are trying to prove our valuation wrong?
17. Can someone specify a different but lower valuation for our company? What reasons can be cited to prove that lower valuation?

18. How can we counter this lower valuation of our company?
19. How the businesses are valued in our industry? Are we valuing our company in a different way or using a new method? Why?
20. How is it calculated in other industries? How is it different from our industry?
21. What are the reasons for this difference?
22. Do we have any existing company in our industry, which is already valued by market, to prove our valuation? How this market valuation can help us?
23. Is our valuation, in any way, different from market valuation? If yes, why? How can we counter the specified argument, proving our business valuation wrong?
24. For our business, what is the valuation of tangibles and what is the valuation of intangibles?
25. How the valuation of tangibles is calculated?
26. How the valuation of intangibles is calculated? Would this valuation of intangibles be considered as respectable in our industry?
27. Can we define a method of valuation which would be acceptable to all?
28. If such a common method is not found then how are we going to justify a common valuation to all stakeholders and investors?
29. Have we checked our data and reasoning to prove the correctness of our valuation?
30. Is any new method of valuation evolving, which is not widely used, but can help us to prove our valuation?
31. Can we get the professional help from the market to help us with the best possible valuation of our business? Can these professionals also help us to get investors for us?
32. How would we be valued in different countries? How would that affect us in raising money?

33. How the different accounting practices of the countries would affect the valuation of company? How other MNCs do it?
34. How the market demand for our offering in different countries would affect the valuation?
35. Who are the best and most reputed experts in the market who can give the accurate estimation of company valuation? How can they help us?
36. Are we connected with them? How can we reinforce our valuation through these experts?
37. What are the pros and cons of connecting with them? As we may have several people opposing them in the market.
38. What can we do to get connected with them?
39. Are we on the right track and using the precise resources to get the best valuation for our company?
40. How the amount raised would be used?
41. Why this is an attractive investment plan for investors?
42. What is the exit plan of inventors?
43. What is the payment schedule and collateral (for debt)?

About Author

Anshuman is an entrepreneur and investor and has been instrumental in nurturing many successful companies. He has created of several successful companies in various domains. He is also involved in supporting development of several other companies. In business, his interests lie in cutting edge technologies and innovative services.

His guidance has helped many businessman, investors and entrepreneurs to succeed in their businesses. He has also supported several entrepreneurship cells and incubation centers.

He is an engineer and a management graduate. He can be reached at anshuman.connect@gmail.com

www.ingramcontent.com/pod-product-compliance
Lightning Source LLC
Chambersburg PA
CBHW071521180526
45171CB00002B/335